未来へつなぐ
平和のウムイ^{思い}

沖縄戦を生き抜いた14人の真実

創価学会沖縄青年部 編

第三文明社

沖縄本島に上陸するアメリカ軍。上陸用の船などが水平線のかなたまで見える(1945年4月、アメリカ沿岸警備隊撮影)

US troops landing on the coast of Okinawa. Landing craft and warships cover the ocean out to the horizon. (April 1945, photo by US Coast Guard)

沖縄戦から70年の「6・23沖縄慰霊の日」に合わせ、「世界平和の碑」の前で開催された、沖縄青年平和主張大会「OKINAWA サマーピースフェスタ2015」の模様（2015年6月20～21日、恩納村の沖縄研修道場）。かつてこの場所には米軍の核ミサイル「メースB」の発射台があったが、いまは平和の砦として生まれ変わった

Commemorating the 70th Okinawa Memorial Day on June 23, OKINAWA Summer Peace Festa 2015 (June 20 and 21, 2015, Okinawa Training Center in Onnason) took place in front of the Monument to World Peace. What was once a launch pad for the US nuclear missile Mace B is now a fortress for peace.

未来へつなぐ平和のウムイ(思い)——沖縄戦を生き抜いた14人の真実

はじめに

一九六四年（昭和三十九年）十二月二日、那覇市の創価学会沖縄本部で学生部会が開催されました。そこには、沖縄を訪れていた池田大作SGI（創価学会インタナショナル）会長が出席。当初の予定にない突然の出席でした。居合わせた学生たちは皆、会長とは初めての出会い。

会長は学生たちに沖縄の平和建設の使命を真剣に語りかけました。

「沖縄の歴史は、悲惨であった。宿命の嵐のごとき歴史であった。だからこそ、ここから、幸福の風が吹かねばならない。平和の波が起こらねばならない。

また、みんなの中から、沖縄の出身であることを誇りとし、日本を、世界を背負うような大人材が出なくてはならない……」と。

その日に、会長が小説『人間革命』の執筆を沖縄の地で開始していたことは、それから九年後に世に知られるようになりました。

「戦争ほど、残酷なものはない。戦争ほど、悲惨なものはない……」

この平和宣言ともいうべき一節から始まる小説『人間革命』の起稿の日が十二月二日だったことを知った創価学会沖縄青年部のメンバーは、当時、準備を進めていた戦争体験集第一号『打ち砕かれしうるま島』の発刊準備にますます力を注いでいきました。

小説『人間革命』の主題は「一人の人間における偉大な人間革命は、やがて一国の宿命の転換をも成し遂げ、さらに全人類の宿命の転換をも可能にする」です。

この人間革命の思想を、日本中、世界中に伝え、沖縄から平和の波を起

こしていくことを目的に、創価学会沖縄青年部は沖縄戦の継承運動を展開してきました。

七四年（昭和四十九年）六月から七九年（同五十四年）六月までの五年間に五冊の戦争体験集を発刊。さらに、八一年（同五十六年）からは、体験者に「沖縄戦の絵」を描いていただく運動を開始し、約七百枚の絵を収集してきました。八五年（同六十年）以降、「沖縄戦の絵」展を各地で開催し、平和の心を発信してきました。

この平和運動を永遠に継承していくため、戦後七十一年が経過した今、新たな青年世代による、新たな反戦出版『未来へつなぐ平和のウムイ（思い）――沖縄戦を生き抜いた14人の真実』を発刊する運びとなりました。

女性と子どもが戦争の一番の犠牲者であり、その真実を浮き彫りにするために、今回は女性に焦点を当てました。さらに、取材した体験者のほとんどが当時成人に満たなかった方々です。

そして、沖縄戦全体の実像をこの一冊で伝えられるように、できるだけ多角的な体験を収録しました。激しい砲弾の嵐の中、必死に逃げ惑った体験。家族を日本兵に射殺された体験。ひめゆり学徒隊の生存者の体験。座間味島や慶留間島での強制集団死の体験。沈没した対馬丸の話。当時、日本に強制連行されてきた朝鮮人軍夫についての目撃証言や、慰安所で炊事係として働いていた方の体験も収録させていただきました。

また、沖縄戦のことは海外ではほとんど知られていない現状があります。紛争やテロが世界各地で絶えない現代において、沖縄戦の真実を発信していくことは極めて重要であると考えます。世界各国の方々に伝えていくために、今回の出版では証言の全文英訳も収録しました。

戦争を体験していない私たちにとって、戦争体験の取材は想像を絶する話の連続でした。取材を進める中で「もう思い出したくない」と言われる

方に、今回の出版の意義を説明し、無理を申し上げて語っていただくことともありました。また、取材しようとしても、高齢で話ができなくなっている方もいれば、取材の数日前に亡くなられた方もいらっしゃいました。その一方で九十歳を過ぎても、はっきりと話ができる方もまだまだ生存されており、今が戦争体験を直接聞くことのできる最後の時期に差し掛かっていることを肌身で痛感しました。沖縄戦の継承は、私たち創価学会青年部の使命であり責務であると強く自覚した次第です。

最後に、沖縄戦の本質は権力の魔性の暴走であったことを確認しておきたい。

沖縄戦当時、慶良間諸島に米軍が上陸した日からちょうど五十年後にあたる九五年(平成七年)三月二十六日。恩納村の沖縄研修道場で行われた第一回沖縄県記念総会の席上、池田SGI会長は次のようにスピーチしてい

ます。
「ただ一点、将来のために一緒に確認しておきたいことがある。それは、沖縄戦ほど『日本の権力の魔性』を雄弁に証明したものはない、という事実である。なぜ、あれほどの犠牲者が出たのか。それは、『日本の本土を防衛するため、なるべく長く、米軍を沖縄に釘付けにしようとした』戦略からであった。初めから、そういう作戦であった。沖縄の国土は本土のために『捨て石』にされ、『盾』にされ、『手段』にされたのである……」
『権力の魔性』は、残酷である。そのことを一番、心の奥底で、肌身で知っておられるのが、沖縄の皆さまである。私が小説『人間革命』をこの地で書き始めた理由も、沖縄が一番『権力の魔性』によって苦しめられた国土だからである。小説『人間革命』は、『民衆による〝権力の魔性との闘争〟』を描く小説だからである」と。

以上のことから民衆を軽んじる権力の魔性の存在を忘れないことが大切であり、沖縄戦の真実を若い世代が学び残していくことは、平和建設への着実な歩みになると確信します。
本書を世界中の多くの方々にお読みいただき、平和のための手がかりとなれば、これ以上の喜びはありません。

二〇一六年九月

沖縄青年平和委員会委員長　砂川　大悟（だいご）
沖縄女性平和文化会議議長　中　由乃（なか　よしの）

沖縄戦略年表

一九四四年(昭和十九年)

- 三・二二　大本営、第三二軍(渡辺正夫中将)を設立
- 四・一二　第三二軍、沖縄本島、伊江島に航空基地建設を命令
- 七・七　　サイパン陥落
- 八・一〇　渡辺司令官に代わって、牛島満中将、第三二軍司令官に着任
- 八・二二　対馬丸が米潜水艦の攻撃を受け、悪石島付近で沈没。学童約七八〇人を含む一四八〇人超が犠牲に
- 一〇・一〇　米機動部隊、南西諸島全域を空襲。那覇市を無差別攻撃し、九〇％が焼失
- 一一・九　第三二軍、首里城地下に司令部壕構築を開始
- 一二・一四　第三二軍、南西諸島警備要項に基づき沖縄本島中南部在住の老人、女性の北部疎開と戦闘能力のある者の戦闘参加を県に要求

一九四五年(昭和二十年)

- 二・九　　米軍、沖縄侵攻作戦(アイスバーグ作戦)を発令
- 二・一〇　島田知事、中南部住民一〇万人の北部疎開を指示
- 三・二三　米機動部隊、沖縄本島への大規模攻撃を開始

- 三・二四 米艦隊、沖縄本島砲撃を開始
- 三・二六 米軍、座間味村三島に上陸。慶留間島、座間味島で住民の「強制集団死」発生
- 三・二七 米軍、渡嘉敷島など三島に上陸
- 三・二八 渡嘉敷島で住民の「強制集団死」発生
- 三月末 沖縄の二一の中等学校の生徒が「鉄血勤皇隊」「学徒隊」として戦場に動員
- 四・一 米軍、沖縄本島西海岸(北谷・読谷村)に上陸
- 四・三 米軍、沖縄本島を分断。北部方面と南部方面に部隊を展開
- 四・一九 米軍、宜野湾・浦添の防衛戦を突破
- 五・五 日本軍、総攻撃に失敗。沖縄戦の敗北決定的に
- 五・二二 第三二軍司令部、首里放棄と南部方面への撤退を決定
- 六・一九 第三二軍の牛島司令官、「最期まで敢闘し悠久の大義に生くべし」とする最終命令
- 六・二三 牛島司令官が自決
- 六・二五 大本営、沖縄作戦の終結を発表
- 七・二 米軍、沖縄作戦の終了を宣言
- 八・一五 日本が無条件降伏
- 九・七 日本軍残存部隊と米軍間で降伏調印式

目 次　未来へつなぐ平和のウムイ（思い）──沖縄戦を生き抜いた14人の真実

はじめに ……… 3

沖縄戦略年表 ……… 10

砲弾の直撃で失った左腕と青春　徳元文子 ……… 17

壕に瀕死の母を残し、捕虜となる　玉城　信 ……… 39

日本兵に命じられるまま外に出た父は爆死　渡久山スミ子 ……… 55

「泣き声を聞いて育つ木」の下で爆死した親友	大城　梅 …… 67
目の前にいた男子学生の首が一瞬で飛んだ	泉川美恵子 …… 81
腐乱死体を踏みながら逃げた	前原静子 …… 107
強姦されそうになり、川に飛び込む	与那嶺勝枝 …… 123
わが家のお墓で銃殺された二人の妹	嘉数廣子 …… 137
死んだ母親に寄り添い、泣き続ける幼子	梶原玲子 …… 151
「対馬丸」で教え子を死なせた母の苦悩	神山洋子 …… 169
ひめゆり学徒隊として負傷兵を看護	新川初子 …… 183

覚悟を決めて集団死の現場へ

　　　　　　　　　　　　　田中美江 ……… 209

慰安所「南風荘」の炊事係になって

　　　　　　　　　　　　　兼島キクエ ……… 229

集団死で生き残った私

　　　　　　　　　　　　　山川久子 ……… 247

むすびにかえて ……… 262

［編集注］「集団自決」という言葉について、「自決」には「国に殉ずる崇高な死」という意味があり、国が起こした戦争のために強制的に死に追いやられた一般市民の死にあてはまらないとの観点から再検討する動きがあります。そこで、本書では特定の地域共同体や家族などが集団で「死を選択せざるを得なかった」という意味から、「強制集団死」もしくは「集団死」と表現した個所があります。ただ、証言内容の本文については、証言者が使用している言葉を尊重しそのまま採用しています。

口絵写真提供

共同通信社（沖縄本島に上陸するアメリカ軍）

聖教新聞社（OKINAWAサマーピースフェスタ2015）

砲弾の直撃で失った左腕と青春

徳元文子 さん

とくもと・ふみこ　一九二四年(大正十三年)八月生まれ。沖縄戦当時、農協に勤務。父は防衛隊に召集され、母を中心に糸満で暮らしていた。「山部隊」の本部壕に連行され、水汲みや炊事に携わる。残る家族は日本兵に壕を追い出され、後に妹以外、全員が死亡。友人四人と壕にとどまるが砲弾が命中し、左腕に大怪我を負い、後に切断することになる。友人らは死亡した。戦後、妹と再会。配給所の仕事に就いて懸命に働いた。九十二歳。糸満市米須在住。

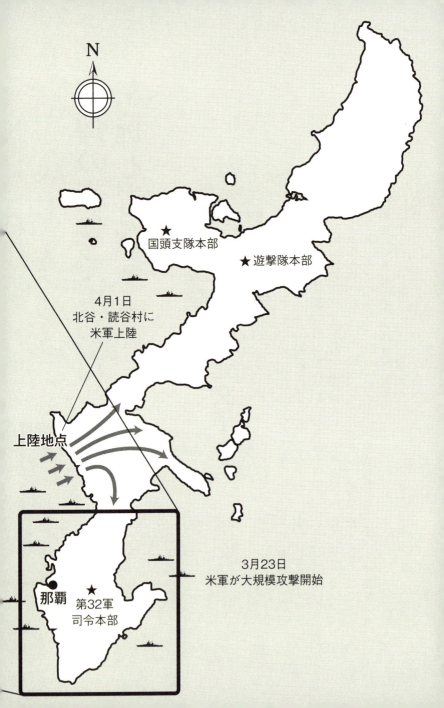

徳元文子さんの記憶

苦労をともにした友人に励まされ、血まみれになりながら逃げた

 私はこれまで、何度も「沖縄戦の体験を語ってほしい」と頼まれましたが、お断りしてきました。思い出したくない過去の記憶を引きずり出した後は、二〜三日、胸が痛み、何も手につかなくなるからです。
 私は沖縄戦で左腕を失いました。それ以上に多くのものを失いました。戦争ほど愚かなことはありません。けれど、世界ではその戦争がまだ続いています。そのことを考えると、たまらない気持ちになります。
 そこで、少しずつですが、中高生などに戦争体験をお話しするようになりました。

 私が住んでいた糸満はサトウキビの栽培が盛んな地域で、広大なサトウ

キビ畑が広がり、近くに製糖工場もありました。二十歳の私は、農協に勤めていました。

昭和十九年頃、沖縄に関東軍の「武部隊」が入ってきて、陣地構築や飛行場造りを始めました。村の男たちは飛行場造りに徴用され、泊まり込みで働きました。

私たち二十五歳以下の未婚の女性も、小禄飛行場の番屋（宿舎）に泊まり込みで一週間ほど働きました。私たちは、ダイナマイトで爆発させた後の石ころをザルに入れて頭に載せ、運ぶのです。そのうち、学生たちも駆り出され、シャベルを担いで、村をあげて飛行場造りを急ぎました。

昭和十七年のミッドウェー海戦で、航空機を発着させる航空母艦の大半を失った日本は南西諸島を航空基地とする必要に迫られ、沖縄の十五カ所に飛行場を造る計画だった。

その後、「武部隊」は台湾に移動。代わって満州から「山部隊」がやってきました。

昭和十九年十月十日に、初めての大規模な空襲（「一〇・一〇空襲」）があり、那覇の町は全焼。それからも度々、空襲があり、サイレンが鳴るたびに防空壕へ走るようになりました。

私たちのいた糸満・米須の村は次第に戦争の影が色濃くなり、学校も兵隊の宿舎になったため、生徒たちは、"樹の下教室"で勉強せざるを得ませんでした。

婦人たちは、当番制で宿舎の学校で兵隊の炊事の手伝いをしました。農協勤めの私は、軍へ供出する野菜の出荷に追われていました。

昭和二十年三月二十三日早朝、上の姉と近くの井戸に水汲みに行った帰

り、海の方からグラマン機が二十〜三十機、編隊を組んでやってくるのが見えました。

そして、見渡す限り青々と広がるサトウキビ畑に次々と焼夷弾が落とされたのです。サトウキビ畑はたちまちバチバチとすごい音をたてて燃え広がりました。

これが、私が最初に見た「戦争」でした。

恐怖で足がもつれる中を、どうにか家にたどり着きました。家族はすでにわが家の防空壕へ避難していました。姉と私も壕へと急ぎました。

翌日、昼過ぎから本格的な攻撃が始まりました。海上からの「ドーン、ドーン」という激しい艦砲射撃で壕からは一歩も出られません。

夜になって、ちょっと静かになったので家に食料を取りに戻ると、村落は砲撃で焼けたり壊れたりして、まともな家は一軒もありませんでした。

仕方なく壕に戻りました。数日後、夜に助役さんが来て、「アメリカ軍は八重瀬町港川から上陸するから北部の山原（名護から北の方面）に避難するように」と告げると、村の人たちは、われ先にと避難して行きました。
私たちの家族も、数日かけて与那城まで逃げましたが、避難する壕が見つからず、結局、昼は山の中に隠れ、夜になって、再び村落の壕に戻りました。村では足の悪いお婆さんが二人残っていて、戻って来た私たちを見て大喜びしていました。心細かったのでしょう。

ある日、壕に二〜三人の日本兵が来て、「若い者が親と一緒にいて戦に勝てるか。軍に協力しろ！」と言って、私は連行されたのです。思えば、これが私の不運の始まりでした。
連れて行かれたのは山城村落。「山部隊」の本部壕でした。
そこでは、すでに友達四人（カズさん、ノブさん、シゲさん、フミさん）が働

いていました。私が加わったことで、二人ずつのグループに編成され、残りの一人が当番で炊事係をすることになりました。

昼は艦砲射撃や空爆があるので、壕の中で臼に入れた玄米を杵で突いて精米する「玄米撞き」、夜になると外に出て水汲みや野菜とりをしました。

水汲みは、壕から三百メートル程離れた泉まで行くのですが、ここにはあちこちの壕から友達が来ているので、久しぶりの再会が楽しみでした。

でも、どこの部隊に居るといった内容を話すと、「スパイ行為」とみなされ、怒られるので話もできません。その監視のための兵隊もいました。

夜の作業は、ときには危険なこともありました。敵の飛行機から照明弾が落とされると、地上からも「ボン、ボン」と照明弾が上がり、あたりは真昼のような明るさになります。それを合図に、どこからかグラマン機が現れ機銃掃射するのです。

ある日、夜の作業に出かける前のことです。壕の入り口で空を見上げて

いたら、東北の方角から日本の特攻機が現れました。すると、たちまち数本の敵のサーチライトに照らし出され、またたく間に高射砲で撃ち落とされてしまったのです。

それ以来、特攻機を見ることはなくなりました。代わりに、敵のグラマン機が空いっぱいに編隊を組んで飛ぶのが見えました。少しでも人の動くのが見えると、たちまち低空飛行で降りてきて、「バリバリ」と機銃を撃つのです。「用足し」に行くのも、命がけでした。

海を見ると、島の近くには米軍の上陸用の船艇。その後ろには軍艦、沖のあちこちに航空母艦が見えました。敵艦は私たちのいる米須海岸だけでなく、東海岸、西海岸もいっぱいだったそうです。

ある晩、私は、荷物を整理していた兵隊から声をかけられ、「これから部隊が移動するので、いらなくなったからあげるよ」と、婦人用の細い革

ベルトとブリキの裁縫箱を手渡されました。この革ベルトが後になって私の命を救ってくれたのです。そのときは、ただ珍しくて、いつもモンペの上から締めていました。

翌晩、闇の中を大隊は出発。これでやっと親元に帰れると喜んでいたら、
「当分、壕からは出るな！」と残留兵に言われました。私たちが壕を出て、敵に通報するのではないかと疑って、「監視する兵隊」を残していったのです。

四〜五日して、「球部隊」が入ってきました。
私たちは髭の准尉の前に並ばされました。私は勇気を出して、「戦闘が激しくなっています。どうせ死ぬなら、親と一緒に死にたいので帰してください」と、哀願しました。
すると、髭の准尉が怖い顔をして、「山部隊には協力して、球部隊には協力できんというのか！」と怒鳴るのです。

後で分かったのですが、私たちのことはいつの間にか「軍の申し送り」として、勝手に次の部隊に引き継がれていたのです。

この「球部隊」には北部の「護郷隊」(中学等の学生で編成された「鉄血勤王隊」に対し、それ以外の少年で編成された部隊) という十四～十五歳の少年兵が二～三人、交じっていました。弾薬箱を運ぶ彼らの細い肩を見ていて、「こんな子どもまで狩り出さなければならなかったのか」と、かわいそうでなりませんでした。

「球部隊」が来て数日もたたないうちに砲撃が激しくなり、山城村落の壕を捨てて移動することになりました。移ったところは、米須城跡の裏の武部隊の掘った壕で、横穴もあり堅固な壕です。

そのうち、首里(しゅり)が敗れ、負傷兵や避難民が私たちの壕にも逃れてきて、壕は野戦病院となりました。次々と運ばれてくる負傷兵が多すぎて入りき

れず、山の裾野に横たわっている負傷兵もたくさんいました。
看護婦はいなくて軍医が一人だけ。壕の中での手術は悲惨なものでした。麻酔薬がないので、負傷した手足をそのまま切断するのです。大声で暴れ泣き叫ぶ負傷兵を、周囲の兵隊が押さえ、上官らしい人が「それでも貴様、軍人か!」と、失神するほどビンタするのです。
ちょうど雨期で、壕の中は泥と負傷兵の血と切断した手足にたかる蛆虫で、ひどいありさまでした。私たちの足の指の間は、赤く爛れていました。

米須城跡の壕に着いたばかりの頃、大雨で飲料用の泉に泥が流れ込み、炊飯ができなくなったので乾パンが支給されました。
「二人の姉の子どもたちにあげて、芋と交換してこよう」と、私は家族のいる壕に行きました。姉たちには男の子が一人ずつおり、上の姉の子は四歳、下の姉の子は一歳になったばかりで、いつも背負われていました。

29　徳元文子

壕の前では、四～五人の兵隊に、うちの家族がちょうど壕から追い出されているところでした。父が防衛隊に召集される前に、「残していく家族のために」と、何日もかけて掘った壕です。

びっくりして、「私の家族です。うちの壕から追い出さないで！」とお願いすると、逆に「なんで、（家族を）疎開させなかったんだ！」と怒鳴られました。

兵隊の剣幕に、姉の子も怯えてベソをかいています。母と姉たちはそのまま壕を追い出されていきました。

後から聞いたところでは、あの後、「どうせ死ぬなら、空気のきれいなところで死のう」と、海岸の自然壕に向かったということです。海岸の壕は米艦から目につきやすいのです。

母たちは、そこで亡くなったことを知りました。あのときが、私と家族との最後の別れでした。

六月二十日頃だと思います。「アメリカの戦車が山を越えた」と言って、軍に解散命令が出ました。

六月二十三日、牛島司令官が自決。

兵隊たちは各自、勝手に壕を出て行き、残ったのは私たち女性五人だけでした。今度は、監視兵もいません。

私たちは、「壕から出て別々に死ぬより、壕の中で一緒に死のう」と、話し合いました。

翌日からは、「ドーン、ドーン」と爆弾が壕に当たって破裂する音がするたびに壕は激しく揺れ、天井から土や石ころが落ちてきました。私たちは生き埋めを覚悟して戸板を一枚敷き、そこに五人で抱き合って

いました。そんな日々が三日ぐらい続きました。食料もなく、天井から滴り落ちる数カ所の雫を飯盒の蓋で受け、それを一つにまとめて、みんなで喉の渇きを癒やしました。

爆発は何日も続き、ある日、砲弾の一つが壕の中に命中したのです。覚えているのは、頭がボーとして気を失ったことだけ。しばらくして意識が戻ると左手が重く、血がドクドク出ているのに気づきました。私は、少しでも出血を止めようと左手を頭の上におき、血の出ているところを右手で強く握りました。

暗闇の中で、フミさんが豆ランプをつけ、私の腰の革ベルトを外して、そのベルトで傷口の根元をきつく縛ってくれました。

見ると、フミさんも足に怪我をしています。シゲさんは眉間に豆粒大の爆弾の破片が刺さって起き上がれません。私は、シゲさんは助からない、

32

と思いました。

ここに居れば、敵がやって来ます。私は「シゲさんと一緒にここに残る」と覚悟を決めたのです。

すると、カズさんが、「あんたの怪我は手でしょ。歩けるんだから、出よう！」と、励ましてくれたので、夜を待ってシゲさんを残して四人で壕を出ました。

しかし、血がしっかり止まっていなかったので、途中で歩けなくなってしまい、もう、起き上がることもできません。喉は焼けるように渇いていました。

夜が明けてくると、私は、「思いっきり水を飲んで死のう」と、みんなと別れて、這ってクラガー（暗川＝洞窟内を流れる地下水）まで行きました。クラガーには五〜六体の白骨化した死体が沈んでいました。でも、そのときの私は、何も感じなくなっていました。

徳元文子

手で川の上の水を払い、下の方の水をおなかいっぱい、飲みました。三カ月余りの穴倉生活で煤けた手足もきれいに洗い、清々しい気持ちで岸に上がりました。

そのとき、訳の分からない言葉が聞こえてきました。見ると、四～五人のアメリカ兵が私を指さしながらやってくるのです。今まで歩けなかったのに、びっくりして立ち上がり、十メートルぐらい逃げました。すると、前の方からもアメリカ兵が来たのです。

その場にヘタリ込んだ私を取り囲み、兵隊は、「傷の手当てをする」というようなことを身振り手振りで伝えてきましたが、私は、「どうせ強姦されるんだ」と思っていたので、「イヤイヤ」と、首を振り続けていました。

米兵の一人が、ヒョイと私を抱き上げ、ジープに乗せました。私は生きた心地がせず、ジープの中でブルブル震えていました。

収容所に着いてびっくりしました。そこには百人余りの人たちが居たからです。

すぐに、野戦病院で手術が行われました。左腕は真っ黒く腐っていて、傷口には白い蛆虫が蠢いていました。私の左腕は切り落とされたのです。しばらくはショックで、「死なせて！」「殺して！」と泣き叫ぶ日々が続きました。周囲からは「あの子は気がふれている」と、言われていたようです。

手術から一週間ほどで、私は宜野座（国頭）の病院に移されました。初めての包帯交換です。包帯を解くと、いつ入ったのか、切断した傷口にたくさんの蛆虫が巣くっていました。

傷も次第に良くなってきたので、突き出ている骨の再手術をすることになり、その後、私の腕は付け根から切り取られました。

徳元文子

八月十五日のことは、忘れることができません。朝から米兵が銃を「バン、バン」撃つので、歩ける日本人負傷者はみな逃げて行きました。

私は、てっきり「日本軍が逆上陸してきた」と思っていました。ところが、戻ってくる日本人が、みな泣いているのです。聞いてみると「日本が負けた」と。私も、ベッドのシーツを頭から被って泣きました。その日が八月十五日、「日本の終戦の日」だったのです。

その後、友達の消息も分かりました。壕に残ったシゲさんは、そのまま亡くなり、一緒に壕を出たカズさんは、私と別れてから破傷風に罹り、亡くなったそうです。フミさんとノブさんも発見され捕虜になった後、ずいぶんたって病死されました。

私の家族は、妹だけが石川で生きていると聞き、会いに行きました。左腕が無くなった私を見て、妹は号泣しました。そこで、私は両親と二人の姉と子どもたちが亡くなった様子を聞いたのです。

私は、急にこういう体になったので、人の視線が怖くて外出ができませんでした。
　特に戦後、若い女性たちがお化粧して軍関係の仕事に出かける姿を見ると、自分が惨めでやりきれませんでした。
　けれど、「いつまでも気にしてばかりではいけない」と、勇気を奮い起こしました。そして、配給所の仕事を紹介してくれた人があったので、仕事に就きました。
　「生まれながらの体じゃない、戦争のためこうなったんだ！」と開き直り、今日まで生きてきました。身体障害の方には申し訳ないですが、そうとでも思わなかったら生きるのが辛かったのです。

壕に瀕死の母を残し、捕虜となる

玉城 信 さん

たましろ・のぶ 一九二〇年（大正九年）十一月生まれ。糸満・宇江城の裕福な農家に生まれ、両親と十一人兄弟で暮らしていた。沖縄戦当時は二十四歳で、夫が亡くなったため、子を連れて実家に戻っていた。「一〇・一〇空襲」の後、日本軍に実家を追い出されたため壕に避難するが、そこも追い出される。父と妹が砲弾の爆風で即死、母は怪我を負い破傷風に。弟は日本兵に射殺され、残る家族は米軍の捕虜となる。二歳の長男の笑顔だけが希望だった。九十五歳。糸満市在住。

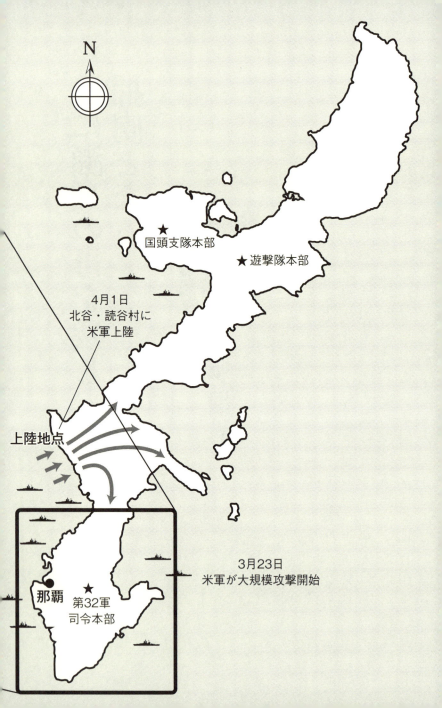

玉城 信さんの記憶

日本兵に射たれた弟は、転げ回りながら死んでいった

糸満・宇江城にある私の実家は大きな農家で、芋、サトウキビ、野菜などを手広く作っており、春になると国頭から小作人が、何人も手伝いに来ていました。

家族は両親と、男五人、女六人の兄弟で、私は三女です。

私は二十一歳で結婚し、すぐに男の子が生まれましたが、その子が一歳になった頃、主人がヤギ汁を食べて食中毒に罹り、亡くなってしまいました。主人の遺言で、「自分が死んだ後は、実家に戻って子どもを育ててほしい」と言われていたので、私は子どもを連れて、また娘時代の賑やかな生活に戻ってきたのです。私の長男が増えて、宇江城の実家に戻ってきたのです。

昭和十九年十月十日のこと（一〇・一〇空襲）は、ハッキリと覚えてしま

す。空いっぱいにたくさんの飛行機が悠々と飛んでいるので、てっきり友軍機だと思って見ていたら、軍の放送で「敵の飛行機ですから逃げてください」と言うではありませんか。「変だな？」と思っていると、どんどん焼夷弾を落としているのです。

びっくりして村落の人たち全員と、ガマ（自然壕）に逃げ込みました。このガマは、「東ガマ」「中ガマ」「西ガマ」と、三つ繋がった大きな自然洞窟で、中をクラガーが流れていました。

夕方になって、飛行機も見えなくなったので村落に戻ってみると、村は焼夷弾にやられて焼け野原になっていました。三十余軒あった家屋で残っていたのは、私の実家と四〜五軒だけでした。

実家は新築したばかりの大きな二階建てで、二本の煙突が目印の、村でも評判の建物でした。

玉城　信

「一〇・一〇空襲」の数日後のことです。

突然、友軍が屋敷に来て、「本日よりここは軍が使用する!」と言うと、私たち家族全員は追い出されてしまったのです。

しかも、戦況が悪化し、島民動員令で長兄は防衛隊にとられてしまい、すぐ下の十八歳の妹は、山部隊に看護婦として召集され、後に戦死しました。

長兄の嫁と長女、次女が中心となって、まだ小さかった三男、四男、五男を連れて国頭に疎開しました。

そして、残された両親と私とすぐ下の十九歳の弟（繁三）と、一番下の双子の妹（照子と美代子）の六人だけの壕生活になりました。

昼間は、外に出ると敵機から狙われるので、蒸し暑い壕の中で横になっていて、夜になるとご飯を炊いたり、食料の芋掘りに出かけたりしました。

この頃は、昼間だけでなく、夜遅くまで首里(しゅり)を攻める砲弾の音が続いて

夜中の三時頃、近所の友達二人と一緒にうちの畑に芋掘りに行きました。普段は、夜中でもときおり砲弾の音がするのに、その夜は不気味なほど静かだったことを覚えています。

芋を一カ所に集め、ネギやキャベツなど、ほかの野菜もとっていこうと移動したとたん、名城の浜より艦砲射撃が始まりました。まだ夜も明け切らないうちの砲撃です。集めておいた芋を運び出す余裕もなく、走り出すと、私たちのすぐ後ろに砲弾が落ちました。爆風で倒れたところに、土砂や石ころが落ちてきます。「もう、ダメか！」と思いましたが、起き上がって走り出すと、今度は二十メートル手前に爆弾が落ち、あわててうつ伏せになって難を逃れました。

こうして、私たちは必死で壕に逃げ帰ったのです。

玉城 信

そんなことがあってからは、夜でも外出はしないようにして、芋掘りなどは父がやり、私は壕の中で「玄米搗き」をやっていました。

あるとき、その大きなガマにも友軍が来て、「ここは軍が使用するから（島民は）出て行け！」と。

屋敷も取り上げられ、壕まで追い出されては、いるところがありません。一緒に追い出された人たちは、あっちでウロウロ、こっちでウロウロしているうちに弾丸に当たって死んだり、死にきれず苦しがって転げ回ったり、悲惨なありさまでした。辺りには死体もゴロゴロと転がっていて、それが腐ってすごい悪臭がしています。

私たち家族六人は父に連れられて、再び実家に戻りました。わが家に着くと、上官らしい男が、「なぜ戻ってきたのか！」と怒鳴りました。父は必死の形相で、「ここは私の家だ！」と怒鳴り返しました。その剣幕に驚

46

いたのか、「他を探すまで二～三日は、いてもよい」ということになりました。

部屋は、私たちが住んでいた頃とはまったく違って、台所まで負傷兵が横たわっているため足の踏み場もありません。

結局、父がツルハシとスコップで家の近くに穴を掘り、家族で入りました。

そこへ兵隊が来て、「貴様たちは何もできない。戦っているのは我々だ！」と言うと、そこからも追い出しました。きっと、私たちが目障りだったのでしょう。

父は、「どうせ死ぬなら、うちの畑で死ぬ！」と言って、畑に隣接した友軍の陣地近くに穴を掘り、家族はそこに入りました。

どこにいてもおなかがすきます。食べ盛りの弟や双子の妹たちのためにも、私は長男を背負って遠くの畑まで芋やサトウキビを探しに行きました。

47　玉城 信

私が出かけている間に、友軍の陣地に砲弾が落とされました。穴の中は暑いので、ちょうど外に出ていた父と、父に抱かれた双子の妹の照子が爆風で即死。母は首に爆弾の破片が入り、大怪我を負いました。穴の中で寝ていた次男の繁三だけが無傷でした。近くにいた人が、亡くなった父と妹の照子を畑に埋めてくれました。

陣地近くは危険なので、私たちはこの穴を捨て、裏山に空の壕を見つけて移りました。

爆弾の破片で首に怪我を負った母は、首も肩も腕も、痛々しいほど赤く腫れ上がり、傷口にはウジが湧き出しています。でも、薬も何もありません。ウジを摘まんで取り除くくらいしか、私にできることはありませんでした。

しばらくして、防衛隊から戻った長兄がやっと私たちを探し出してくれ

ました。
そして、「捕虜になったら戦車で轢き殺される。ここは危ないからすぐに逃げよう」と言うのです。
母は、首から腕にかけて腐りかけています。私は、「母さんを置いては逃げられない！」と泣きながら兄に訴えました。
ところが、母が息も絶え絶えになりながら、「信！あんたにはかわいい子どもがいるじゃないか。子どものためにも生きなさい。安全なところに早く行け！私のことなんて心配するな！」と言うのです。
そのときです。「バーン」と銃声が聞こえたかと思うと、すぐ下の弟・繁三の「痛いよ〜、助けて〜」という声が聞こえました。
繁三は五歳のときに脳膜炎に罹り、知的障害を抱えていました。でも、色白で目のクリッとしたかわいい子で、いつも歌を歌っていました。父もそんな繁三をとてもかわいがって、馬を一頭与え、その馬の牧草刈りは彼

の役目となっていたのです。いつも鼻歌を歌いながら、草を刈っていた弟でした。

このとき、弟は自分たちのいる壕から屋敷の母屋へ水を飲みに行ったようです。歌をやめない繁三に腹をたてたのか、知的障害なので面白半分にやったのか、兵隊が小銃を抜いて繁三のおなかにむけて撃ったのです。おなかを押さえて、畑で苦しがって転げまわる繁三を見ていられませんでしたが、上空には敵機がいるので、私たちは助けたくとも助けに行けないのです。

苦しくて泣き叫んでいる弟の大声で、いまにも敵機が降りてくるのではないかと、兵隊たちは不安がり、黙らせるために弟めがけてさかんに発砲し、とうとう、弟は射殺されてしまいました。

あまりの悲惨なできごとに、私は長男を抱き締めたまま呆然(ぼうぜん)としていました。

それを見ていた長兄は、直接、兵隊に怒りをぶつけられないので、突然、鎌を持ち出すと、狂ったように「うちの家族は絶対、捕虜にならない！捕虜になるぐらいだったら、みんなの首を切り、私も死ぬ！」と叫び、暴れ出しました。鎌を振り上げている兄を、私は必死で止めました。

「繁三はスパイと疑われて射殺された」と思ったのか、「そういうこと」にして怒りを爆発させたのか、長兄はかわいそうなほど取り乱していました。

気持ちのやり場もなく、怒り狂った長兄は、一夜明けてようやく冷静になりました。

その直後に、米軍の戦車がやって来たのです。壕に入っていた私たちは、出されました。

私は、破傷風に侵されている母がいることを、一生懸命、身振り手振りで米兵に伝えましたが、伝わっているかどうかさえ、分かりません。

米兵は、「早くトラックに乗れ！」と命令しました。私は、「母さんと一緒にここに残る」と言いましたが、長兄が、「残っていると殺されるぞ！早く行くぞ」と急き立てます。

「必ず連れに来るからね。待っていてね」と励まし、まだ息のあった母を壕に残したまま、私たちは捕虜になりました。

収容所は佐敷にありました。その後、しばらくたってから佐敷収容所から母を残してきた糸満・宇江城の壕に行ってみましたが、すでに母はいませんでした。母とは、それっきりでした。

悲しいこと、辛いことが続いた一年でしたが、唯一の救いは母が言ったように、私のもとに生まれてきて、もうすぐ二歳になろうとする長男の笑顔でした。

状況の過酷さを知る由もなく、時々、意味もなくニッコリするその笑顔に、私たちは生きる勇気をもらったような思いでした。

母との思い出はたくさんあります。十一人の兄弟の中で、私が一番、「母さんっ子」でした。実家は裕福でしたが、子だくさんで小作人も大勢来ていたので、母はいつも忙しそうでした。

だから、自然と私が小作人へのお茶を持っていく係になり、また、朝、学校に行く前に必ず、各部屋の掃除をするのも私の役目でした。母はそれを黙って見ていてくれ、いつも、「あんたがいないと難儀するよ」と。学校から帰ると、母はよく豆を潰して島豆腐を作っており、私はその手伝いをするのが楽しみでした。母と話ができるからです。私が六年生になった頃、島豆腐作りの手を止めて、母が、「信には上の学校に行かせてやりたい」と言ってくれました。でも、一番下に双子の妹たちもいたので、私は、「行かんでいい、いつまでも（母の）そばにいる」と答えました。

53　玉城　信

日本兵に命じられるまま外に出た父は爆死

渡久山スミ子 さん

とくやま・すみこ　一九三九年（昭和十四年）十月生まれ。沖縄戦当時は五歳で、那覇市若狭町に両親と兄、妹と暮らしていた。人力車の車夫だった父にかわいがられ、人力車に乗せてもらったり、肩車をしてもらったりした。糸満の通りで額に爆弾の破片が刺さる大怪我を負うが、日本兵の手当てにより助かった。避難しているとき、日本兵に銃を突き付けられて外に出た父は、爆弾を受けて即死する。母は一人で父の亡骸を埋め、花を供えた。七十六歳。沖縄市在住。

渡久山スミ子さんの記憶

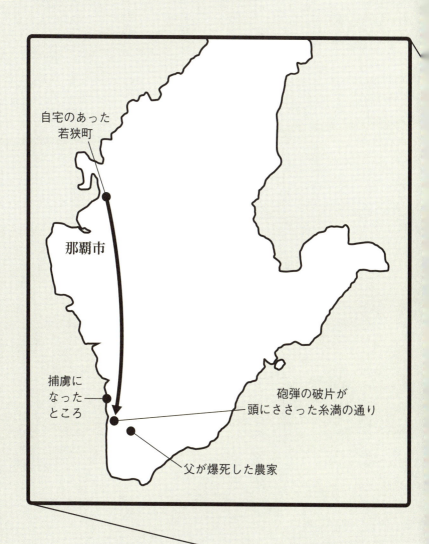

爆弾の煙のなか、
私を探す母の叫び声が聞こえた

　当時、五歳だった私がなぜ、こんなに明確に沖縄戦のことを覚えているかというと、その後、母が父の思い出とともに、いつも詳しく話してくれたからなのです。いわばこれは、私と母・具志堅カメとの証言です。

　戦争が激しくなる前、私たち家族は那覇の若狭町に住んでいました。毎朝、家の前を食糧部隊が味噌汁、おかず、ご飯などを大きな容器で運んでいくのが見えました。私は窓から、「お汁部隊！」「ご飯部隊！」などと、大声で声援を送っていました。

　家族は、父と母、十歳の兄、五歳の私、それに一歳になったばかり妹の五人。戦争が激しくなり、私たち家族は父に連れられて、砲弾の飛び交う

58

なか、南部方面（糸満）に逃げました。食べ物も飲み水もありません。喉が渇くと母が溜め池を見つけて両手で水を掬って飲ませてくれた。私は夢中で飲でいましたが、その池には死体が首から浸かっていたり、浮いていたりしていたそうです。

やっと、糸満の農家の一軒家に家族で身を寄せました。そこには数家族が避難していて、それぞれ家族ごとに固まって休んでいました。でも、子どもたちは親とは関係なく、ひとかたまりになって走り回っていました。子どもの数だけでも二十人以上はいたと思います。

三〜四日たったある日のことでした。父と兄が庭で夕涼みをしていると、その家に突然、爆弾が落とされたのです。モウモウと煙が立ち込めるなか、母は一歳の妹を背負ったまま半狂乱で

私を探しました。倒れたり、うずくまったりしている子を一人ひとり抱き上げては、「ウリンアラン！（これではない）、クリンアラン！（この子でもない）」と叫びました。必死で私を探す母の、この声だけは、私も不思議と覚えています。

そして、母は私を見つけ出すや、破壊された家の中から引っ張り出しました。振り返るとゴウゴウと音を立てて、その家は燃え上がっていました。一緒に遊んでいた多くの母のおかげで、私は間一髪で助かったのです。子どもたちが、そこで亡くなったと聞きました。

糸満の通りは、あちこちから流れ込む人でごった返していた。その人ごみに向かってまたも爆弾が落とされ、多くの人が亡くなりました。転突然、爆弾の破片が私の額の左側、髪の生え際に突き刺さりました。がっている死体や、血だらけで逃げる人々の中を、私は痛さと恐怖で泣き

60

叫びながら逃げました。
　そのとき、近くの壕から飛び出してきた日本兵が、「泣いているその子を、ここに連れてこい！」と怒鳴りました。
　父と兄とは離れ離れになっていました。妹を背負い、私の手を引いた母は、その日本兵に殺されると思ったそうです。
「兵隊の命令に従わないと殺される」というのは、当時、当たり前になっていた。母は観念して私の手を引いて壕に入って行ったそうです。
　震えの止まらない母に兵隊は、「その子を台の上に寝かせなさい」と。てっきり殺されると思っていたのに、私の額に刺さった爆弾の破片を抜き取り、傷口を消毒すると薬まで塗ってくれたのです。
　破片を抜いたときにたくさんの血が飛び散りましたが、頭を包帯でグルグルと巻いて、しっかり結んでくれた。母は逃げている間じゅう、巻いた白い包帯が私の目印になって見つけやすかったと言います。この包帯は、

61　渡久山スミ子

後に捕虜になって治療を受けるまで外れなかったので、傷口が悪化せずに済みました。
軍医さんだったのか衛生兵さんだったのか、今は知る由もありませんが、この兵隊さんに私は生命を助けられたのです。

私たち母子はさらに避難を続け、ある村の入り口で、偶然に父と兄に再会することができました。心細かったのでしょう、母は泣いて喜び、私たちはそのまま一軒の農家に避難。再び家族全員が揃った翌朝、一人の日本兵が銃を構えたまま飛び込んできました。

そして、父に銃を向け、「米兵がどこまで来ているか、見て来い！」と命じたのです。

「言う通りにしないと皆殺しにされるかもしれない」と、父は黙って出て行きました。

母は嫌な予感がしたそうです。その直後、爆弾の破裂する大きな音がしました。母は、とっさに父のことが心配になって飛び出すと、父はうつ伏せで地面に倒れていました。即死だったといいます。命令した兵隊はすでに姿を消していた。

母は父の遺体を、焼夷弾で開いた近くの穴に引きずり入れ、さすがに持っていた手拭いを顔にかぶせて、直接、土がかからないようにして埋めました。

その様子を、向かい側で何人かの日本兵がニヤニヤ笑って見ていたそうです。母はこの話になると、「殺してやりたいほど憎かった」と、いつも怒りで身体を震わせながら語るのです。

一人で父を埋め終わった母は、「戦争が終わったら、必ず骨を拾いに来ますからね。それまで待っていてくださいね」と言い、目印になるようにと、何本ものハイビスカスの枝を切って父を埋めた場所に植えたのです。

突然の父の死は、私にとっても辛いものでした。父は、戦争前は人力車の車夫でした。子煩悩で陽気な父は、娘の私をとてもかわいがって、花街にお客さんを迎えに行くときは、人力車に私を乗せていくのです。とてもオマセな子だった私は、お店に着くとお囃子に合わせて見よう見まねで踊ったりしたそうです。

お人形遊びなどには見向きもしない私に、父は花街のお姐さんの使うような口紅や白粉を買い与えてくれました。それは私の宝物でした。

もう一つ覚えているのは、父に肩車をされて小禄まで行き、抱えられないほどのたくさんのホオズキを畑からとってきてもらったことです。

突然、父を失った母は三人の子どもを連れて、避難する大勢の人たちと必死になって逃げ回りました。昼は藪に隠れ、夜になってから移動しまし

糸満の海岸を逃げたことは、おぼろげながら覚えています。波打ち際を、土手に身を押し付けるようにして移動するのです。その土手の上を、米兵を満載した車両が何台も通って行きました。

けれど、結局、私たちは糸満の海岸付近で米軍に捕まり、捕虜になってしまいました。連れて行かれた米軍施設の中で、上半身裸になった米兵たちがキャッチボールやバスケットボールをしている光景を目にしたときは、いままでの自分たちとのあまりのギャップに、「私たちは何だったのだろう？」と気が抜けたようになりました。

そのときに、子どもたちだけ集められ、缶から直接、手づかみでもらったクッキーの美味（おい）しかったことは忘れられません。

その後、小さな村に移動させられると、掘っ立て小屋に家族ごとに住み、畑を耕して数カ月暮らしました。

戦争が終わって、小禄の叔父さんの家に戻った母は、すぐに親類の人たちと一緒に父の眠る場所に行きました。必ず分かるようにと、屋敷の角に開いた穴に埋めたからです。村の名前や屋敷の名前は母が覚えていました。行ってみると、私たちを待っていたかのように、そこには真っ赤なハイビスカスの花が鮮やかに咲き誇っていました。

「泣き声を聞いて育つ木」の下で爆死した親友

大城 梅 さん

おおしろ・うめ　一九二六年(大正十五年)七月生まれ。糸満で八人兄弟の末っ子として生まれる。十七歳のとき結婚し、翌年、長男を出産。親友に夫の甥を紹介し、二人は結婚する。親友の家族を含む三家族十四人で糸満の壕に避難したが、親友は爆弾の破片が刺さり亡くなる。激しい襲撃のなか、命からがら逃げた。米軍の捕虜となり、石川の収容所に送られた。九十歳。糸満市在住。

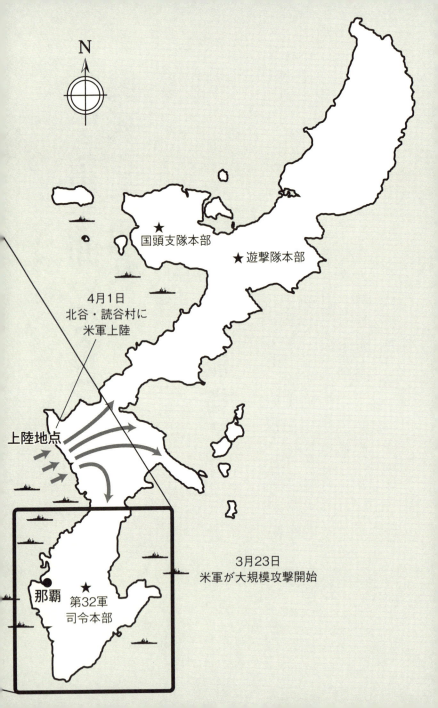

大城 梅さんの記憶

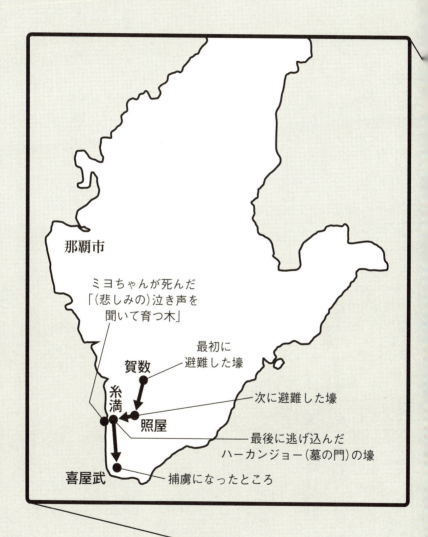

赤ん坊が泣くと、壕を出なければならなかった

私は八人兄弟の末っ子で、上は全員、男です。上原家（旧姓）で初めての女の子として生まれました。

初めての女の子だからやさしく育てられたかというと、そうでもなく、父が厳格だったので、夜の外出は絶対にさせてもらえないなど、とても厳しく育てられました。ですから、私の青春は結婚してからでした。

子ども時代は、いつも裸足で砂浜を走り回っていました。怪我をするようなものは、どこにも落ちていないほど美しい砂浜でした。

結婚は十七歳のときです。「早く結婚しないと、内地の軍需工場に強制的に行かされるよ」と、父に脅かされ、私は本気にしました。まわりは、誰彼なしに兵隊にとられるような雰囲気だったのです。

夫は十歳年上で近所に住んでおり、日頃から気性も知っていたので父も大変、気に入っていたところ、私を「嫁に欲しい」と頼まれたので、二つ返事で承知したそうです。

結婚式は、沖縄のしきたりにのっとって、近所でしたが、夫の家から数人が提灯を下げて「嫁を迎えに来る」という儀式を行いました。わが家は布団と琉球反物で新しい着物を作り、私はそれを持って嫁入り。

戦時中なので披露宴というほどではありませんが、近所の人や親しい人たちが三十人ほど集まってくれ、お祝いの豆モヤシの和え物をたくさん作って、庭で月桃の葉に盛って出し、食べてもらいました。

結婚してからも嫁ぎ先と実家が近所なので、ついつい実家に顔を出していると、父から「いくら近いからといっても一度嫁いだら、実家にはそう

71　大城　梅

簡単に帰ってこないものだ」と怒られた。

翌年、十八歳で長男・功を産みました。ところが、出産十八日目に、海軍の夫は駆逐艦に乗船し、戦地へ。嫁ぎ先には夫の両親と出征前の学生の四男がいて、私は子どもの世話に追われていました。

しょっちゅう、グラマン機が飛んで来るようになり、爆撃が始まったので、私たちは賀数の壕に入ることにしました。

実母が長男・功を背負って、私が食べ物の入った桶を頭の上に載せ、実父がクワを担ぎ、夜を待って壕に急ぎました。父のクワは、誰かが亡くなったときに埋葬するためのものでした。

照明弾が打ち上げられると、その明かりを目印に爆撃機が飛んできます。建物や壕への人の出入りが見えると、その建物や壕めがけて爆弾が落とされるのです。賀数の壕も危なくなったので、照屋の壕に逃げ込みました。

ところが、照屋の壕もたちまち標的にされ、とうとう糸満のハーカンジョー（墓の門）という壕に入りました。中は大きなお墓を壕にしたところで、階段状の三層になっており、一番上にはお墓がありました。

私たちは二層目に入りましたが、中は遺骨がたくさん散らばっていたので、その上に藁ムシロを敷いて寝るしかありませんでした。

その壕には、実家の家族、嫁ぎ先の家族、大城ミヨちゃんの嫁ぎ先の家族の三家族十四人が入っていました。

私と大城ミヨちゃんとは、糸満国民学校時代の同級生でとても仲良しで、家も近かったので、学校への行き帰りはいつも一緒。ミヨちゃんは活発で明るい性格なので、とても気が合いました。

日本では、まだバレーボールがあまり知られていない頃で、担任の女の先生が、「こういう球技がある」と言ってルールを教えてくれました。新聞紙を丸めてボールの形にして、それを布で包んでバレーボールの代用品

を作り、それを手で打ち上げて練習。馴染みがない球技なので誰も興味を示しませんでしたが、ミヨちゃんが真っ先に、「やりたい！」と言ったので、私も一緒に始めたのです。

風紀係の先生に、「そんな敵国の球技などをやって！」と注意されましたが、ミヨちゃんと私は、「放課後なんだから、いいじゃない！」と平気でした。

私は結婚するとすぐに、夫の甥っ子にミヨちゃんを紹介し、二人は結婚。彼女は私と同じ「大城」の姓になり、すぐに男の子が生まれました。ミヨちゃんのところは八カ月、うちの功は一歳と、年がほとんど変わらなかったので、顔を合わせるといつも、夫の消息や子どものことを話し合いました。

ミヨちゃんの夫は現地召集で防衛隊に取られ、飛行場造りなどで島内を

移動していました。

当時、赤ちゃんのために配給で練乳やミルク菓子のような補助食が配られていたので、「あと、どれくらい残っている？」などと、よく情報交換し合ったものです。

ミヨちゃんとはずっと一緒の壕でした。三番目のハーカンジョーの壕に入ってやっと落ち着いたと思った、ある日の夕方、ミヨちゃんの長男がムズがり出し、次第に大声で泣き始めました。

当時は、赤ん坊が泣いたら母親は赤ん坊を抱いて壕を出なければなりません。

「泣きやまない赤ん坊を壕の中で兵隊が殺した」という話さえ、あちこちで聞かれていたのです。うちの功が泣いたら、私もやはり出ていたと思います。

ミヨちゃんは長男を抱いて、五メートルほど先の大きな木の下に座り込みました。

この壕が「墓の門」と呼ばれていたので、その前の大きな木を、周囲の人たちは「(悲しみの)泣き声を聞いて育つ木」と呼んでいました。

その大木の根元に腰をおろすと、ミヨちゃんはオッパイを出して、泣いている赤ん坊に乳を含ませました。赤ん坊は少しおとなしくなりましたが、また突然、火の付いたように大声で泣き出しました。

私が驚いて顔を上げて見ると、ミヨちゃんの額に爆弾の破片が刺さっていて血が顔面をダラダラと流れていたのです。即死でした。ほんの一瞬の出来事で、赤ん坊は一口のお乳も吸う間がなかったと思います。

ミヨちゃんの死体が上空から見えるのか、敵機が次々と飛んできた。壕の中にいたミヨちゃんのお母さんが飛び出してきて、ミヨちゃんの遺体を

運び、赤ん坊は小学四年生の義妹が背負って壕を出ました。

このときの敵の襲撃は激しく、皆、自分が逃げるので精いっぱいでした。

かわいそうなことに、この赤ん坊は逃げているうちに栄養失調で亡くなったと聞きました。

逃げる途中、私の周りに三度も爆弾が落ち、そのたびに「今度こそダメか！」と思いましたが、三度とも不発弾だったので、私は死なずに済んだのです。

途中、小学五～六年生ぐらいの男の子が、母親が亡くなったのか、大声でお母さんの名前を呼びながら逃げていました。

その子のさげている飯盒（はんごう）を見て、食べ物が入っていると思ったのでしょう、日本兵が飯盒を取り上げようと飛びかかったのです。その子は、取られまいと必死に抵抗するのですが、日本兵はその子を殴（なぐ）ったり蹴（け）ったりして、とうとう取り上げてしまいました。みんな自分が逃げるので精いっぱ

大城　梅

いで、誰も助けてやる人はいませんでした。

こうして、私たちは喜屋武岬の壕に逃げ込みました。逃げ込んで何日もたたないうちに、壕の入り口に米兵が来て「出テコイ！」「出テコイ！」と呼びかけます。
「女たちは捕まったら（米兵に）強姦されて殺される」と聞かされていたので、私たちは鍋の底の煤を顔に塗って男の子のような格好をしていた。壕の中に、一人の負傷した日本兵がいて、「こうなったら手榴弾で全員自決しよう」と喚き出しましたが、父が、「そんなことを勝手に決めるな！」と言って、腰に挟んでいた手拭いを白旗代わりにして、「大丈夫だから、私の後に付いてきなさい」と先頭に立ち、壕から出ました。壕の中にいた十人余りの人たちも後に続いて捕虜になった。その後、私たちは喜屋武から石川の大きな収容所に送られました。

糸満のロータリーの近くには、いまでも「(悲しみの)泣き声を聞いて育つ木」はそのまま残っています。そこを通るたびに、青い格子柄の着物を着て、赤ん坊にお乳を含ませていた、親友のミヨちゃんの姿を思い出すのです。

目の前にいた男子学生の首が一瞬で飛んだ

泉川美恵子さん

いずみかわ・みえこ　一九二八年（昭和三年）一月生まれ。助産婦学校の学生だったが、沖縄戦の年、十七歳で結婚。西原村翁長で新婚生活を送り、艦砲射撃が激しくなると家族十六人で壕に避難した。攻撃により家族が一人、二人と亡くなるなか、戦火を逃れるため南風原村、新垣、喜屋武岬など、皆で移動を重ねる。戦争が終わった後も、それを知らずに大勢の避難民とともに逃げ回った。八十八歳。浦添市在住。

泉川美恵子さんの記憶

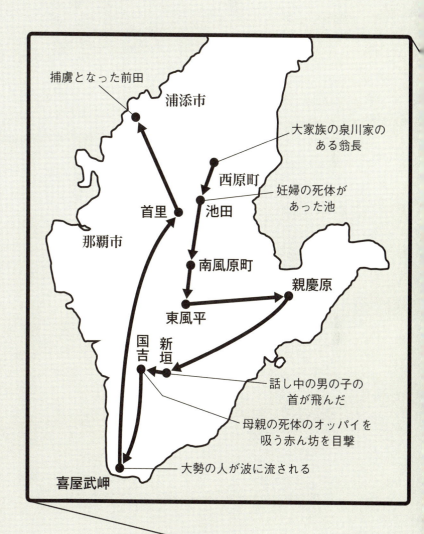

助産婦学校時代の医療器具を使い、壕で赤ん坊を取り上げる

一九四四年(昭和十九年)十月十日。私は那覇の若狭町に下宿し、三キロほど離れた大城産婦人科の助産婦学校に通っていましたが、その日は、たまたま嘉手納(かでな)の友達の家にいました。

明け方、空襲警報のサイレンが鳴ったので急いで壕(ごう)へ避難すると、空は敵の飛行機でいっぱい。音は聞こえませんでしたが、爆弾が花火のようにきれいだったことが、目に焼き付いています。しばらくすると、那覇の空が夕焼けのように真っ赤に染まったのです。「一〇・一〇空襲」でした。

十日ぐらいして、私は下宿に洋服を取りに戻った。周囲のほとんどの家は焼失していましたが、なぜか私の下宿だけは無事でした。

翌年、私は十七歳で結婚。「産めよ！　増やせよ！」という国の政策で、「兵隊が足らなくなるから、子どもを産ませるために早く結婚を！」というわけです。

四歳年上の夫・寛清の叔父さんの家に私が下宿していたことが縁で、「寛清の嫁に」と言われ、結婚しました。沖縄では、女の子は十五〜十六歳で結婚するので、十七歳の私は遅い方でした。

私の実家はコザの高原で、農家です。母は私が十四歳のときに他界しており、夫の母もまた、すでに亡くなっていました。戦時中ということもあって結婚式は行わず、サキムイ（結納式）を行うことに。

夫の家のある西原村翁長から高原まで六キロあります。私の実家まで、夫の父親が戦地に行っているので、長男タンメー（爺さん）が結納金を、三人の叔母さんたちが頭にご馳走を入れた桶を載せて、歩いて来てくれました。

85　泉川美恵子

わが家からは父と妹（下の弟たちは学校に行っていた）、夫の泉川家からは長男タンメーと三人の叔母さん。私たち夫婦を入れて八人でサキムイは行われました。

といっても、夫と私がお膳を前に並んで、盃を交わしただけです。前日、近所の姉さんたちに作法を教えてもらいました。私はモンペ姿、夫は軍服でした。恥ずかしくて、式の間中、私はとなりの夫の顔を見られんかったです。

祝い事は二時間ほど続き、その後は、皆で西原村翁長までの六キロを歩き、私は泉川の家に嫁入りしました。

泉川家の先祖は首里を警護するお侍の家系です。そのためか、男性は穏やかで親切。女性は美人で上品な人たちばかりでした。

私が嫁入りしたとき、お屋敷には長男家族と次男家族が同居しており、私は「長男家系の次男の嫁」という立場です。

86

それぞれの家の男たちは戦争に行っていて、長男タンメーと次男タンメー以外は女と子どもばかり。子どもは六人いました。一番小さい子どもは二歳で、丸首シャツに半ズボン、丸刈り頭がかわいかったことが印象に残っています。

次第に、海上からの艦砲射撃が激しくなってきていた。夫は、農林学校の青年師範部の学生だったので出征前の講習を受け、私も夫の出征準備に追われていました。

けれど、夫の配属が決まっていなかったので、結局、夫も家族と一緒に壕に避難することになりました。二家族合わせて総勢十六人でした。

米軍上陸（四月一日）から二週間ほどたった頃、朝、飼っていたヤギを潰しました。夕方までかかって自宅でヤギ汁を作り、私とナエ姉さん、ヒデ姉さんの三人で大鍋のヤギ汁を家族が避難している壕まで運びました。

87　泉川美恵子

高台の家から、左下にある壕に向かって降りて行くと、私たちの壕の上にたくさんの兵隊が立っていました。薄暗かったので、その兵隊たちが私たちに手を振っているように見えたのです。

「お～い。ヤギ汁を炊いたよ！　降りといでえ。食べて、食べて！」と、私が呼びかけると、足元で「プシュ、プシュ」という変な音が三回ほどしました。

「あれ、あの人たち、なに投げたかね？　なんか合図したみたいだね」夕方で人の顔が判別できるか、できないかの暗さ。それでも「お～い、お～い」と、私たちは呼びかけました。

すると、またもや「プシュ、プシュ」という音が。それは、次第に多くなってきたのです。

「ウリヒャー（驚いた時の悲鳴）、アメリカー（兵）だ！」と姉が叫ぶと同時に、私たち三人はヤギ汁の大鍋をひっくり返して逃げました。

そのときは気がつきませんでしたが、私たちの隠れていた壕の上には、ちょうど馬乗りのような格好で敵兵が大勢いたのです。

気づかれないように壕に戻ると、私たちは一刻も早く、ここから出ることにしました。音を立てても、立ち上がっても敵兵に気づかれてしまいます。闇に紛れて、老人、子どもから一人ずつ這って壕を出ました。私たちは突然、戦闘に巻き込まれてしまったのです。

私の前を這っていた次男タンメー（爺さん）が「プスッ」という音と共に、急に動かなくなりました。少し体を起こしたところを見つかって、撃たれたのです。一声もあげず、即死でした。

次男タンメーは、私が嫁入りしたばかりで心細いときに、「うんじょうび（艶があってきれいな髪の毛）だね」と最初に声をかけてくれたこともあって、親しみを感じ、頼りにしていました。でも、悲しんでいる余裕さえあ

りません。心で祈りながら、無言で壕を脱出。身内が殺されたことで、全員の心に恐怖が走りました。

西原村翁長から一晩中歩いて、深夜、池田に到着。あちこちの壕の中で避難民が火を焚いているらしく、かすかな明かりが漏れています。

十五人の大家族なので一緒に入れてもらえる壕が見つからず、子どもたちだけを分散して壕に入れてもらい、大人たちは木の下や川のそばに隠れました。

艦砲射撃は夕方の五時頃に終わるので、それがやむと、荒れた畑に行きカンダバー（芋の茎）やマーミ（インゲン豆）など、食べられるものを探しました。

ところが艦砲射撃で樹木も草も根こそぎ吹き飛ばされて、地肌が剝き出しになっているのです。せめて、子どもにだけでも何か口に入れてやりた

いと思い、必死で探し回りました。

大きな池の脇を通ったとき、おなかが膨らんだ三十代ぐらいの妊婦の死体を目撃しました。おそらく池に水を飲みに来て、撃たれたのでしょう。結婚したばかりの私にとって、辛い光景でした。上半身裸で、膨らんだおなかの辺りが露出していました。私は上着を脱いで、死体のおなかの胎児に掛けてやり、飛ばないように端に石を置きました。このときまでは、まだ死者を悼む気持ちがありました。

池田には二～三日いましたが、飛行機からは焼夷弾、海上からは艦砲射撃、その上、戦車砲まで飛んできます。私たちは、追われるようにして南風原村に向かいました。

昼は砲弾が飛んでくるので移動は夜だけです。子どもたちは怯え、小刻みに震えていましたが声を立てると銃弾が飛んでくるので、二歳の子さえ

泣きもせずに黙々と歩いていました。

艦砲は硬い音がします。戦車砲は重い音、飛行機の爆弾は落ちるときまでは音はしませんが、落ちると「バーン」という弾ける音がします。小銃は遠くへ飛ぶときは「ビューン」という音がしますが、近くでは「プスッ、プスッ」と、ほぼ音がしないので怖かったです。

南風原村では、どの道にも死体が転がっていました。私たちは食べ物を持っていないので、悪いとは思いましたが、死体が持っていた米を詫びながら持ち去りました。その米を炊くために、水を探さなければなりません。やっと見つけた池や川は、どこも死体が浮いていて、水は血の臭いがします。炊き上がったご飯は、血の臭いがしました。

南風原村で二十日ぐらい過ごした頃、砲弾が飛んでくる中、私たちの壕に「看護婦さんがいると聞いたのですが、子どもが生まれそうなのです」

と、悲壮な顔をした三十過ぎの男性が駆け込んで来た。壕の人たちは私に、「いま出て行くと危ないよ」と止めましたが、私は、「生まれてくる赤ちゃんは待ってくれない。私には弾丸は絶対当たらないから！」と言って壕を飛び出しました。

助産婦学校のときから使っていた鋏、リバガーゼ、メスなどの医療器具を持ってきたので、役に立ちました。

妊婦のいる壕には、布もなければお湯もありません。草の上に上着を脱いで敷き、その上で分娩させました。臍の緒を切り、胎盤を堕ろしましたが、赤ちゃんの体を拭く水も無いので、上着の袖で顔の血をきれいに拭いてあげた。元気な男の子で、産声を聞いたときは本当にうれしかった。

夫婦も泣いて喜んでくれ、お礼に鰹節を一本、いただきました。この鰹節がその後、私たちの飢えを救ってくれたのです。

泉川美恵子

南風原村から二日かけて、東風平に到着。東風平で二十日ぐらいたった頃、壕の入り口に座っていると妙な胸騒ぎがしたので、夫の手を引いて近くのタコツボに移動しました。

タコツボに着いた途端に、壕の入り口付近に爆弾が落ち、中にいた全員が生き埋めに。掘り出す道具もないので、夫と二人で救助を求めて駆け回りました。弾丸の飛んでくる中を、山の上にいた日本兵が五〜六人、駆けつけてくれ、家族を次々と掘り出しましたが、壕の奥の方にいたツル姉さんだけは、亡くなってしまいました。大家族の女性たちの中で、一番の美人でした。遺体は、近くに穴を掘って埋葬しました。

爆弾で壕が埋まったので、私たちは玉城に向かいました。一晩かかって、親慶原に到着。

皆、乞食のような格好でした。親慶原は避難民でいっぱいで、ちょっと

見ただけでも百人以上の死傷者がいた。私たちは昼は壊れた家の石垣や木の下などに二〜三人に分散して隠れ、夜になると固まって移動。この頃は、ほとんど眠った記憶がありません。二日がかりで新垣(あらかき)に着きました。

その新垣で、とても恐ろしいことが起きた。

隣村から農林師範学校へ通う兄弟がおり、名前までは知りませんでしたが、私とは顔見知りで、その弟と偶然、会いました。農林師範学校の一年生で、学生服姿で丸刈り頭に戦闘帽を被っていた。

「姉さん、元気ヤミセーティ?(元気でいらっしゃいましたか?)」

「兄さんは(戦地は)どこ? あんたも危ないからどこかに隠れていなさい」

と、私が言い終わらないうちに、手の平ぐらいの艦砲の破片が飛んで来たのです。

それが彼の首を切断したかと思うと、飛ばされた首と艦砲の破片とが、少し離れたガジュマルの木に、一瞬で張り付きました。

95　泉川美恵子

向かい合って話していた首の無くなった胴体は、しばらく立ったまま痙攣（けいれん）していましたが、そのまま後ろに倒れました。

この頃の私は、精神的にかなりおかしかったと思います。周囲は死体がゴロゴロ転がっている状況。そんなところで立ち話中に突然起こったことなのに、妙に冷静に観察していたのです。

「驚く」とか「悲しむ」という人間的な感情は湧かず、「死ぬのは即死がいいな。苦しまないでいいから……」と、そんなことを考えていました。

新垣には千人ぐらいの避難民がいましたが、そのうちの大半は死んでいました。死体には、蛆虫（うじむし）がビッシリ湧いています。不思議なことに、弾に当たるとハエがたかる前に、すぐに白い蛆虫がモゾモゾと死体から湧き上がるのです。「弾の中に蛆虫を込めて撃っているのでは」、と思うほどでした。

周囲は死体だらけで、その中を海の方へ、山の方へ行こうとする者たちが右往左往していた。死体を跨いだり、足で脇に押しやりながら、戦場を彷徨っているようなありさまでした。

新垣には井戸はなく、小さな池があったので水を汲みに行くと、腹の膨れた死体が四〜五体、ポンカラ、ポンカラ浮いていた。他に水場がないので、しかたなく大人たちはその水を飲み、赤ちゃんや幼い子どもには、「自身のオシッコ」を飲ませていた。

私たちは、新垣から国吉に向かいました。途中、二キロ近くに渡って累々と死体が横たわっている。私たちには死体を脇にどける力も無いので、腐乱死体を踏んで進むしかありません。今なら、ネズミの死骸を踏むことさえ、気持ち悪いと感じるのに、あのときは何の感覚もありません。履いているのは薄い地下足袋でしたが、無感覚

97　泉川美恵子

でした。意識は、ただ前へ進むだけ。人間ではなかったですね。

その途中、道の左側に、母親の死体のオッパイを吸っている生後八カ月ぐらいの男の子を目撃。母親の顔や首筋には、すでに蛆虫が湧いています。紺地に白い井桁模様の着物から出ている、手足の生々しさが哀れでした。余りにかわいそうなので、私は少しだけ立ち止まって見ていました。
　助産婦だった私は、乳児が気になったのでしょう。でも、普通なら抱きあげて連れていくところですが、そのときはそういう気持ちすら起きませんでした。明日は自分が、この母親と同じように死ぬかもしれない、と思っていたからです。

　ようやく、私たちは国吉に着きましたが、ここはすでに米兵だらけでした。

皆で相談して、年寄りと子どもだけ捕虜になることを決めました。長男タンメー、ウメー叔母さんなど大人四人と、六人の子どもたちの十人。タンメーが、薄汚れたふんどしを外して木の枝に結びつけると、それを持ち、皆で米軍のテントの方へ歩き出しました。

五時で艦砲射撃はやんでいましたが、まだ明るい時間でした。

米軍のテントに到着する直前、突然、樹木や岩陰に隠れていた日本兵が、降伏しようとするタンメーや子どもたち目掛けて銃を撃ち始めたのです。

「やめて！」と叫びたくても、声を出すこともできません。ただただ、祈るように見守っていました。幸い、弾は届きませんでした。

残されたナエ姉さん、夫、私、それにヒデ姉さんの四人は、「米兵の手に掛かって死ぬより全員で自爆する」ことにしました。ただし、ヒデ姉さんは親戚ではないので、彼女まで死なせるのは忍びない、ということにな

りました。ヒデ姉さんは、たまたま泉川家に遊びに来ていて、戦が始まったために帰れなくなったのでした。

三人だけで手榴弾を前に置いて、ピンを抜きました。ところが、爆発しません。ずっと雨が降っていたから湿っていたのかもしれません。どうやっても爆発しないので、最後には石に叩きつけましたが、それでも、爆発しませんでした。

私たちは、生き残ったので、ともかく歩きました。

新垣までは炊いたものを食べていましたが、その後はジャングルの中で野草を食べました。水が無いので洗うこともできず、葉を手で拭いて食べていました。尾籠な話ですが、いつの間にか大便をすると、葉を食べたため、おなかの中で孵化し繁殖したのでしょうか。それとも、ウジャウジャと尻から出てくるようになりました。ハエが卵を産み付けた

死体の浮いている水を飲んだので、その中に蛆虫の卵があったのでしょうか。

胃酸でも死なない蛆虫を見て、「私のおなかの中はどうなっているのだろう」と、気味が悪く、しばらくは「蛆虫恐怖症」になりました。

その後、米兵たちが鉄砲を担いで、私たちの隠れているジャングルを探索に来るようになりました。米兵の気配を感じると四人はバラバラになり、わざと腐乱している死体の横に転がって息を止め、死んだふりをしていました。

腐乱死体にはハエがたかり、体液が流れ出していてすごい臭いなので米兵たちも死体のそばまでは来ないのです。銃の先で死体の足や体を突ついて、生きているかどうか調べるだけでした。

数日後、米軍は飛行機からガソリンをまいて、私たちが隠れていたジャングルを焼き払いました。私たちは火を逃れ、夜になってから喜屋武岬に向かうことにしました。

ところが、歩き始めると、どこから出てきたのか、後ろから避難民がゾロゾロとついて来ます。皆、無言。

闇の中を歩き続け、私たちは喜屋武岬に着きました。海岸では、尖った石が地下足袋を通してブスブス足の裏に刺さり、痛くて歩けません。しかも、逃げてきた大勢の人たちでお祭りの人出のような混雑です。栄養失調で体力がないのでしょう、何人もの人が、声も上げず波に流されていきました。

それから何日ぐらい歩いたでしょうか。昼間を避けて、夜だけの移動で北部を目指しました。

線路沿いに歩き、与那原の辺りに来たとき、誰かが鉄条網に引っかかっ

たらしく、「バーン」と照明弾が上がり、一斉に弾が飛んできました。慌てて逃げると、避難民の朝鮮人男性が撃たれ、私の上に落ちてきました。顔の辺りに彼の尻があるので、私は動けません。彼は苦しそうに呻き声をあげ、朝鮮語で何か叫んでいます。その声を目当てに、米兵が至近距離からやみくもに撃ってくるのです。照明弾が上がっているので、動くと私まで撃たれてしまいます。一時間余り銃撃され、彼は絶命しました。彼の呻き声がやんだので、ようやく弾が飛んでこなくなりました。

夜明け前、死体の下から這い出すと、私はいつの間にか一人になっていました。後日、戦争が終わってから、夫とナエ姉さん、ヒデ姉さんとは再会できましたが。

浦添・前田の辺りでは、大勢の敗残兵や避難民に囲まれた。もう、戦争

はとっくに終わっていたらしく、ただ彷徨っているだけの群れのようで、私もその中に入れてもらいました。

十月頃のことです。夕方、隠れていた壕の前に、日系二世が二〜三人来て、交代で「もう戦争は終わった」と説明し、スピーカーで天皇陛下の放送を流して聞かせました。
それを信じて翌日、午後二時頃の再度の呼びかけに応じて、全員、壕から出て捕虜になりました。そのとき捕虜になったのは、百人ぐらいだったと思います。

六月二十三日、牛島司令官自決で組織的戦闘が終わったとされるが、その後も泉川さんは百日余り逃げ回っていたことになる。

大勢の米兵が見物に集まっていた。女性は壕で知り合った一歳年下のユキちゃんと私だけです。パチパチと写真を撮られる中を、二人で並んで、収容所までの道をまっすぐ顔をあげて歩きました。

腐乱死体を踏みながら逃げた

前原静子 さん

まえはら・しずこ 一九三二年（昭和七年）五月生まれ。沖縄戦当時、祖父母、母、兄弟の八人で南城市玉城に暮らしていた。父は「一〇・一〇空襲」で亡くなり、家族は自然壕に避難し、数十人の人々と避難生活を送る。十五歳の兄が母とともに食料を探すなど、家族を守った。家族で移動中に米兵と出くわしたが、祖父が必死で見逃してくれるよう手を合わせると、兵士は立ち去った。家族が励まし合い、一丸となって生き延びた。八十四歳。島尻郡与那原町在住。

前原静子さんの記憶

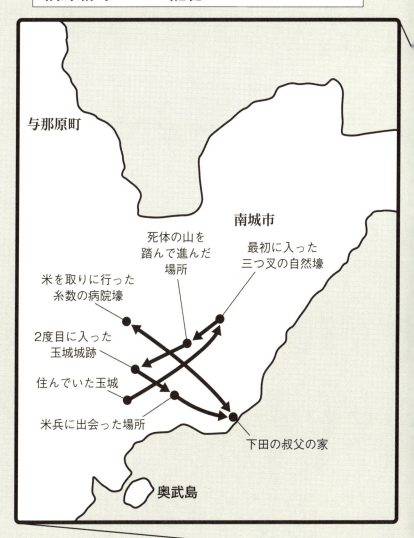

父が乗っていた船が「一〇・一〇空襲」で沈められ、骨も帰って来なかった

沖縄戦当時、わが家は祖父母、母、私たち兄妹五人で暮らしていました。すぐ上の兄・信雄は十五歳、次が長女の私で十三歳、すぐ下の妹・ツル子が九歳、さらに五歳の弟と三歳の妹がいました。

家は農家で、近くに父の兄弟たち二家族が住んでおり、「ユイマール」といって、相互扶助のやり方で、稲を植えるのも、芋を掘るのも、サトウキビから汁を絞るのも、すべて親類で助け合ってやっていました。

家の前はすぐに海で、奥武島という島に、よく潮干狩りに行きました。裏は山になっていて、琉球時代のアマツギ城と呼ばれた玉城城跡があり、城跡近くの大きな沼で妹や弟、友達とよく遊んだものです。

父は前年（昭和十九年）に八重山の飛行場造りに徴用され、帰りの船が「一〇・一〇空襲」によって久米島沖に沈められ、骨も帰って来ませんでした。

「沖縄本島各地から徴用された六百余人の民間人が犠牲になった」と当時、大きく報道された。

そんな父との思い出は、私が最初の女の子ということで、とてもかわいがられ、どこに行くにも私を連れて行ってくれたことです。

たしか、小学校に上がった年のことです。当時、めずらしい汽車に乗って、父と一緒に那覇まで行ったことを覚えています。

父を失ったわが家は、いきなり十五歳の長男・信雄が家長となって私た

ちの面倒を見ることになりました。

私には学校から、一時疎開をしてはどうかとの話がありましたが、母が、「父親がいないのだから、家族は絶対バラバラになってはダメ」と言い、疎開を許しませんでした。

ある日、久米島に飛行場造りに行っていた叔父さんが、「米軍が島に上陸してきた」と知らせに来てくれましたが、そのときはすでに玉城にも海上からの艦砲射撃が始まっていた。すぐに、私たちは家の近くの大きな岩陰に避難しました。

その直後、逃げ遅れた隣の家の叔母さんが爆弾で吹き飛ばされ、死体がガジュマルの木に引っかかったのです。小柄で優しい叔母さんでした。

多くの家と同様、わが家も藁葺き屋根だったので、一発の砲弾で家の半分以上が吹き飛びました。

村落の区長が来て、「あんたのところは三つ叉(また)(親慶原(おやけばる))の自然壕(ごう)に入り

なさい」と指示。当時は、自分たちで勝手に避難場所を決めるわけにはいきません。上からの命令で、入る壕まで指定される。三つ叉の自然壕はかなり遠いところにありました。

梅雨時で土砂降りの中を、信雄兄さんが先頭になり、母がわずかな炊事道具を持って、祖父母が下の弟と妹の手を引いて壕まで歩きました。

「この雨だから、艦砲射撃はないだろう」と、祖父が言っていましたが、土砂降りの雨にも負けないほどの砲撃で、爆弾の破片やら泥がところ構わず飛んできます。その破片が当たって、多くの人が手足をもぎ取られたり死んだりしました。

祖父は額に破片が当たり、顔中が血だらけになり、私も背中に爆弾の破片が入り、痛いのと怖いので夢中になって逃げました。その破片は、いまでも体内に残っています。

艦砲は、最初は低く「コン」と発砲音が鳴り、「ヒュルルル」と唸りながら、落ちて「バーン」と弾けます。弾けるときが一番、恐怖を感じます。子どもの頃、毎日見ていた白い珊瑚礁と青くきれいな海は、米軍の戦艦がびっしり埋め尽くし、こちらを睨みつけているような恐怖を感じました。

三つ叉の自然壕には兵隊はいませんでした。避難したのは、近所の人たち五十～六十人ほどでした。

避難した家族は、自分たちの食料は自分たちで確保しなければなりません。年寄りと幼い弟妹、合わせて八人の食べ物集めが、十五歳の信雄兄さんの肩にのしかかっていました。

夜になって艦砲射撃がやむと、兄は母を励まして食料探しに出て行きます。兄は私より四つしか年が離れていないのですが、すごく大人に見えました。

明け方近くに、収穫の終わった芋畑から残っている親指ほどの小さな芋を探して、戻って来たこともありました。そのわずかな芋を、家族で分け合って食べました。

壕の中では、成人の男の人がいる家族では「馬を潰して食べている」とか、指示を無視して「もっと安全な所を見つけた」といって壕を出ていく家族もいた。

そんな中で十五歳の兄は、必死に私たちを守ってくれた。生き延びられたのは、兄のおかげです。

梅雨時なので、雨が降ると壕の天井から一日中、滴（しずく）がポタポタ落ちてきます。私たちは、着ているものを脱いで絞り、それで身体を拭いて、またその着物を着て、体温で乾かしました。それ以外、方法がなかったのです。

すぐ下の妹のお尻の辺りは、赤く腫れて爛れていた。風呂にも入れず、一日中、濡れているので皮膚病になっていたのです。だんだん、体力も消耗して弱っていきました。「ヒーサン、ヒーサン（寒いよー、寒いよー）」と、か細い声でいつも泣いていました。

夜中、母が暗闇の中、食料の芋などの他に、手探りで蓬の葉を摘んできてはそれを煮出して、痛がるツル子のお尻につけてやっていました。それが唯一の治療だったのです。

また、壕の中は夜になると真っ暗で、手で触らないと物の判別がつきません。その中で、私はカタカタ震えている妹弟を抱いてやりました。異常事態であることが分かるのか、震えてはいますが、二人とも泣くことさえしません。

海の方を見ていると、日の丸の付いた特攻機が米艦に向かって突っ込ん

でいくのを何度も目撃。でも、特攻機のほとんどが米艦に体当たりする前に、花火のように火を吹いて燃えながら海に落ちていくのです。悔しくて体が震えました。

昼は、激しい艦砲射撃で壕から一歩も出ることができません。五十人余りの炊き出しから用便まで、すべて壕の中でするのですから、悪臭が漂っている。そんな三つ叉の自然壕に一カ月ほどいました。

あるとき、中部方面から、米軍の戦車がものすごい速さでこっち（南部）に向かっているという情報が入り、私たちは夜になるのを待って、また雨の中を玉城城跡付近の壕に移動しました。

その移動中のことは生涯、忘れられません。あたり一面、折り重なったたくさんの死体で、山のようになっている。その頃は、履いていた草鞋もなくなり、私は裸足でした。真っ暗な中を裸足のまま、死体を踏みつけて

前原静子

進むのです。暗闇で何も見えませんでしたが、赤ん坊の頭や、その母親の顔を踏んでいたのかもしれません。足の裏を伝ってきた、死体の脇腹のグニャグニャした感触は、今でもはっきりと覚えています。

「(残酷な光景などの)見たこと」や「(悲惨な叫び声などの)聞いたこと」は、時の経過と共に薄れます。しかし、あの「触覚」の記憶は、決して消えることがありません。

一足ごとに鼻につく腐った死体の臭いと、飛び散る体液が足にかかる気持ち悪さ。それでも止まるわけにはいかないのです。地獄があるとすれば、さしずめ、あのときのあの場所でしょう。

しかし、そのときは何も感じませんでした。ただただ逃げるだけでした。

兄と母は、野草とか木の芽とか、何とか食べられそうなものを探しては運んで来てくれた。それで命をつなぎながら、私たちは玉城城跡の壕に、

118

かなり長くいました。

着ている着物は雨と泥に汚れ、原形を留めていません。体にボロ布をまとっているといった格好でした。

やがて、「いつまでもここにいてもしょうがない」と考え、玉城城跡から下田の祖父の親類のところに行くことに。沖からの艦砲射撃もやんでいたので、夕方の少し早い時刻に壕を出ました。

ところが、いくらも行かないうちに、いきなり一人の若い米兵とばったり鉢合わせしたのです。肩から銃をかけたその米兵を見たときは、一瞬、心臓が止まりそうになりました。顔を見たら殺されると思い、私はずっと下を向いていました。

祖父が「孫たちです。女、子どもしかおりません。助けてください」と、必死で手を合わせました。

119　前原静子

言葉が通じたわけではないと思いますが、収容所に連行するのが面倒くさかったのか、あまりのみすぼらしさにかわいそうだと思ったのか、まるで見なかったかのように、その兵隊は、うなずいて立ち去っていったのです。

玉城（たまぐすく）百名（ひゃくな）の近くの下田の叔父の家に着くと、そこも那覇、首里（しゅり）から逃げてきた人でいっぱいでした。ともかく、馬小屋に入り、私たちはそこに陣取りました。

ある日、はるか遠くを米兵に誘導されて東の収容所に向かう、避難民たちの長い列を目撃しました。

避難していた人たちが、「あれは連れて行かれた先で銃殺されるのだ」と話し合っています。今更ながら、あのとき出会った米兵が私たちを見逃してくれたことに感謝しました。

忘れられないことがあります。九月頃だったと思います。食べるものも無く、私たちは芋の蔓などを食べていましたが、「人が逃げた後の壕の中に、食料が残っている」という噂が伝わってきた。

兄が母に、「糸数の病院壕に行ってみよう」と言いました。でも、「壕の中に人が残っていて、食料を取りに入った人が射殺された」という話も聞きます。

かなり前から、祖父母と弟妹たちは空腹でグッタリと横になったままでした。この三カ月余り、弟妹たちはまともな食べ物を口にしていません。何か食べさせてやりたい。

ずいぶん、迷っていましたが、信雄兄さんが母を説得して、病院壕に向かった。

私は不安で、不安で、落ち着きません。二人がなかなか帰って来ないの

で、「何かあったのでは？」と、まんじりともしないで夜明けを待ちました。

明け方近くになって、兄が肩に米袋を担ぎ、満面の笑顔で現れ、母も後ろから頭に米を載せて戻って来たときは、涙がこぼれました。

強姦されそうになり、川に飛び込む

与那嶺勝枝 さん

よなみね・かつえ　一九二九年(昭和四年)八月生まれ。両親と本部村大堂で暮らし、小学生の頃から父の仕事を手伝って家計を助けた。高齢の父、病弱な母の代わりに、軍の作業に徴用される。重労働に耐えたが、米軍の爆撃に遭って家に逃げ帰った。米軍が上陸すると、収容所に入れられ、恐ろしい経験をする。父はマラリアに罹って亡くなり、母のために懸命に食料を探したが、母も栄養失調のため亡くなった。八十七歳。那覇市在住。

与那嶺勝枝さんの記憶

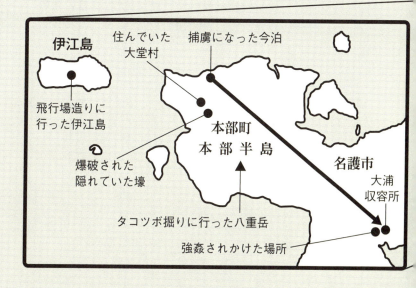

軍の作業に徴用され、辛い労働と寂しさに毎晩泣いた

私は、高齢の父と病弱な母のもと、那覇で生まれました。父は洗濯桶を作る仕事をしていましたが、大酒飲みだったため家計が苦しく、少しでも楽になればと、本部の大堂というところに引っ越しました。

父の作った洗濯桶を、私が頭に載せて本部の町まで売りに行きました。それが、わが家の唯一の収入です。そのような経済状態でしたので、私は小学六年生の途中までしか学校へは行っていません。父は再婚で、子どもは私一人です。

戦争が激しくなると、一家で一人、軍の作業に徴用されるのですが、うちは父が高齢で母も病弱だったので、私が代わりに軍作業に出て大人と一

緒に働きました。私はどの軍作業でも一番年下でしたが、子どもだからと いって手加減なんかしてくれません。むしろ、「何をモタモタしているん だ！」と、いつも怒鳴られるようなありさまでした。

最初の軍作業は、村の七十余軒の家に配属された友軍の食事作りでし た。一軒の家が炊事当番になり、そこで婦人たちが作るのです。当番兵が、 「飯上げ(めしあ)」といって、三食ともバケツを持って取りに来ていた。

それが終わると、伊江島(いえ)の飛行場造りに徴用されました。「東洋一の飛 行場」と言われていましたが、労働環境は悪く、宿舎がないので島の門 中墓(ちゅうばか)（親類一同が入る大きな墓）で寝ました。日本兵が勝手に遺骨を一カ所 に集めて、作業をする女たち二十人余りをそこに入れたのです。そんな門 中墓がいくつもありました。

寝るといっても敷物などないので、地べたにモンペを履いたまま横にな るのです。辛(つら)くて、辛くて、毎晩、「マンマー（母ちゃん）！」と言って泣

127　与那嶺勝枝

きながら寝ました。ここでも、私は一番年下でした。

この仕事は、男の人たちがツルハシで掘り起こした土をネコ車（一輪車）に詰めて運ぶというもの。一カ月余り、伊江島にいて、昭和十九年四月一日に本部港に戻って来ました。

港に着くなり、空襲です。敵機が低空飛行で降りてきて、機銃で撃ったり爆弾を落としたりしたので、多くの人が命を落としました。私は必死で、港の植林してある砂地に腹ばいになって隠れたので、何とか助かることができました。

こうして、私はやっと、大堂に戻って来ました。大堂は盆地で、周囲がジャングルになっているため、高い木があって飛行機が低空飛行できません。その上、木々に隠れた山道は、上空からは見つかりにくい場所でした。そのため、「一〇・一〇空襲」で焼け出された人たちが多く避難して来ていた。

三度目の軍の徴用は、八重岳に陣地を造ることでした。八重岳の高地から名護の町が一望できます。米軍が上陸して下から上がって来たときに、日本軍が穴（タコツボと呼ばれた竪穴）に隠れていて迎え撃つように、その穴を掘るのが仕事でした。山の中に男小屋と女小屋の作業宿舎があり、二十人ほどの女たちに交じって女小屋で雑魚寝しました。

タコツボ掘りは、きつかったです。切り倒した木の根を掘り出し、谷に転がし落とすのですが、斜面での作業なので、万が一、足を取られて転がってくる木の根を避け切れなければ、大怪我をしてしまいます。

ある日、警戒警報が鳴ると同時に、米軍の爆撃機が飛んできて機銃を撃ち始めた。作業中の人たちがクモの子を散らすように逃げ出し、私も敵機に見つからないように警戒しながら、二里の道を一目散に走り、わが家に逃げ帰りました。

あのとき、八重岳で何人亡くなったのかは分かりません。私は二度とそこへは戻らず、そのまま軍作業はうやむやになりました。

村に戻った私は、配給があるたびに、家から一キロ程のところにある配給所に行きました。近くに学校があって、そこは陸戦隊の宿舎だと言われていました。窓からこちらを眺めている若い男たちがいて、私がその建物の前を通るたびに顔を合わせるので、いつの間にか顔見知りになっていました。でも、言葉を交わしたこともないので名前も分かりません。時々、「さらば沖縄〜」という軍歌を何人かで大声で歌っているのが聞こえました。

あるとき、配給所に行くと、係の人からタバコを渡され「陸戦隊の人から、あなたに」と。そういえば、配給所にタバコを買いに来る若い人たちが何人かいました。その中の一人だと思いますが、くれた人が誰なの

か、分かりませんでした。いつの間にか、校舎は空っぽになっていたのです。噂では、全員、伊江島に送られたということでした。
当時は、何でも秘密で、下手に聞いたりするとスパイではないかと疑われます。ですから、最後まで、彼らがどこに行ったのかは分かりません。

やがて、米軍が上陸したという噂が流れ、家にいては危ないので、山の中の小さな自然壕に両親と隠れた。夜になると、わが家に戻って食事を作り、おにぎりや弁当にして壕に持って来て食べました。
あるとき、壕に戻ってみると上空からの爆撃で壕はメチャクチャに壊されていた。昼間、私たちの出入りを偵察機が確認していたのです。壕にいたら即死するところでした。
私たちは、再び他の自然壕を見つけ隠れましたが、毎日、ビクビクしていました。

米軍が上陸すると、米兵が銃を構えて、すぐ近くまで探索に来るようになり、何か話し声がしていたかと思うと、いきなり銃声が聞こえます。すると、壕の中から腕を飛ばされたり、脇腹を撃たれたりした人が、大声で叫びながら飛び出して来るのです。

悲鳴が聞こえても、顔を上げて見ることもできず、石のように固まって、米兵が通り過ぎるのを、じっと待ちました。いつ、自分たちの隠れているところに銃弾が撃ち込まれるかと思うと、恐怖で凍りつく思いでした。

戦争が終わったのか、続いているのかも分からない日々が続きました。

米兵は、二世の通訳を連れて来て、「出テキナサイ。出テキナサイ」と呼びかけていた。

壕に隠れていた村の人たちも、あちこちから出てきた。私と両親も一緒に村の広場に集められ、そこからゾロゾロと列になって今泊(いまどまり)まで歩かされ

132

ました。

　私が、身の回りの物を木桶に入れて頭に載せ、両親と移動していると、突然、米兵の一人に頭の上の桶を叩き落とされた。米兵が、「こんなものを載せていると背丈が伸びないぞ」というようなジェスチャーをしていましたが、私は怖くて拾うこともできず、黙って歩きました。

　今泊で一泊して、翌日、私たちはトラックに乗せられ、国頭の大浦の収容所に送られました。

　収容所に入ってからは、若い女性が米兵に強姦され、殺されて裸で捨てられるということが、よくありました。「あそこの娘も帰ってこない」「あの娘も、突然見えなくなった」と、ヒソヒソと話されていたのです。また、強姦されても騒がないで黙っている女性もかなりいるという噂も流れていた。

大浦収容所では食事といっても小さなおにぎりが一日一個、配られるだけなので、みんな、いつも空腹です。そこで、女性が芋畑などに食料を探しに出たところを狙われるのです。

私も一度、二歳年下のいとこのチョちゃんと、食べられるものを探しに出かけました。左手が山の斜面で、右側がゴウゴウと音を立てて川が流れている場所まで来たとき、突然、ガサガサと音がしたので何気なく山側を見ると、二人の米兵が茂みの中から立ち上がったところでした。

そして、その米兵がすごい勢いで私たちにむかって降りて来たのです。

目を血走らせ、明らかに私たちを襲う気です。

とっさに、「強姦されて、殺される！」と思い、「マンマー（お母ちゃん）」と叫びながら、チョちゃんの手をとって、音を立てて流れている川に飛び込みました。あのときは、火の中だって飛び込んだと思います。それほど怖かった。

ずぶ濡れになった二人は、泣きながら収容所に戻りました。
しばらくして大堂に帰されましたが、家も山も火炎放射器で焼かれ、周りの地肌は黒焦げになっていました。
山の中に掘っ立て小屋を建て終わった頃、高齢の父はすでにマラリアに罹(かか)っており、高い熱が出て、ブルブル震える父を「病院」に連れて行きました。村のはずれに「病院」はありましたが、そこは民家の元豚小屋だったところで薬もなく、その年（昭和二十年）の十一月に、父は亡くなりました。
私は母と二人きりになりました。私たちは、村では耕す畑もなく収入もありません。
ですから、家の中に食べ物はなく、病弱な母は栄養失調で寝たきりになってしまったのです。

私は時々、「戦果」を上げに行きました。当時は、そういう言葉で呼ばれていたのですが、要するに他人の芋畑に盗みに行ったのです。芋を蔓（つる）と抜いてきて、母と二人で食べました。芋は、葉も蔓も全部食べました。食料のない時期だったので、見つかったら確実に殺されます。だから、必死でした。あの時期は、どうやって暮らしていたのか、思い出せないほどです。

母は次第に衰え、一九四八年（昭和二十三年）のある朝、目を覚ますと冷たくなっていました。

生前、「かむしがねんね（食べ物がないから）、ぬち（命）ゆいちかりんな（生きられないよ）」と弱々しい声で言っていた言葉が今でも、耳に残っています。

わが家のお墓で銃殺された二人の妹

嘉数廣子 さん

かかず・ひろこ　一九三三年（昭和八年）七月生まれ。沖縄戦当時は十一歳で、母と祖母、三人の妹と共に本部町新里で暮らしていた。艦砲射撃や空爆が激しくなり、家族六人で丘の上に立つ先祖の墓に避難する。その後、壕に移動しようとしたが二人の妹は銃で撃たれ死亡。自分はマラリアに罹り、もうろうとして動けないほどだったが奇跡的に回復した。沖縄戦終結後、母と祖母もマラリアに罹り亡くなった。妹と二人で野菜や芋を作って売り、力を合わせて生き抜いた。八十三歳。宜野湾市在住。

嘉数廣子さんの記憶

女ばかりの家族のため壕を掘ることができなかった

私たちが住んでいた本部町新里は、本部半島の突端にあるノンビリとした田舎で、村ではサトウキビ、芋、稗、ふだん草を栽培していました。ふだん草は、小松菜のように茎が白く葉の大きな野菜で、炒めたり茹でたりして食べるほか、豚の餌としても利用されていた。家の前は遠浅の海で、白砂の美しい浜辺が広がっていた。

父は私が七歳（終戦の四年前）のときに病気で亡くなり、家では母と祖母（父の実母）と私、それに三人の妹が暮らしていました。

沖縄戦当時、私は十一歳、妹の光子は八歳、恵子は五歳、トシ子は四歳でした。長女の私は、家事はもちろん、母、祖母と一緒に畑仕事を手伝っていました。

四姉妹はいつも一緒で、仕事の合間にはよく妹たちと家の前の海で遊んだものです。母は古着を解いて、私たち四人に手製の水着を縫ってくれました。

海は遠浅なので、私と光子は満潮時に沖の方まで行き、砂地を足の指で掘ると、白ハマグリがたくさん取れるのです。潮が引くと、岩のくぼみで逃げ遅れてバタバタしている魚を手づかみで捕まえます。恵子とトシ子は小さいので、波打ち際で砂いじりをして遊んでいました。皆で家に戻ると、母が白ハマグリは汁に入れ、魚は美味（おい）しく焼いてくれた。

戦争が始まり、海からの艦砲射撃や飛行機からの爆弾投下で、日に日に村は破壊されていきました。

わが家は女だけのため、米軍が上陸すると聞いても、他の家のように「壕（ごう）掘り」ができません。私たちは恐ろしさと心細さで、家から十分ほど

沖縄には、三月(旧暦)の清明祭とお彼岸にはご馳走を持ってお墓に集まり、亡くなったご先祖様と過ごすという風習があります。だから、お墓に行くと父にも会えるので安心できたのです。お墓の中は広い部屋になっていて、入ることができて女家族六人で、ひっそりと隠れていました。
しばらくすると、村の巡査が来て、「ついに米軍が上陸した。ここは危ないから山に避難しなさい」と告げました。
数十キロ離れた本部富士の中腹には友軍の掘った大きくて頑丈な壕があるのです。
母は最初、墓に留まろうとしましたが、「年寄りや子どもがいるのだから、ここにいると殺される。許可を取ってあるから行きなさい」と、巡査は熱心に勧めました。
しかし、二人の妹(恵子、トシ子)は、艦砲射撃の「ドーン、ドーン」と

いう音に怯えてしまって、「どこにも行きたくない。父さんのいるお墓にいる」と言って動かないのです。

そうこうしていると、犬の吠える声が聞こえ、母は妹たちを隠して墓の扉を閉め、急いでその場を離れました。祖母の手を引き、藪や林を抜けて急ぐなかで、うちの墓の方角から激しく吠える犬の声がしたかと思うと、続いて銃声が響きました。その音は、しばらく続きました。

私たちは、直感で妹たちが撃たれたと分かりました。母と祖母は一瞬、「ああ～」と叫んでその場にしゃがみ込みましたが、すぐに皆で泣きながら逃げました。

翌日、艦砲も銃声もやんだ頃を見計らってお墓に戻ってみると、おかっぱ頭の二人は重なるように死んでいました。恐怖で抱き合っているところを撃たれたのでしょう。埋めてやる余裕もないので、二人の上にゴザをかけてやり壕に戻りました。埋めてやったのは四～五日たってからのことで

身内の死に関しては、こんなこともありました。前年の「一〇・一〇空襲」の頃のことです。そのときも、私たちは村の近くの友軍の掘った壕に入っていました。

前方には民間の頑丈な壕があちこちにありましたが、私たちは入れてもらえないのです。

そんな私たちを不憫に思ったのか、叔父が炊事当番の家から炊き出しの食事を届けに来てくれました。

ところが、「おーい、食事を持ってきてやったよ。開けて」と、言い終わらないうちに爆撃機から焼夷弾が投下され、叔父は爆死。焼夷弾が落ちると、四～五メートルもの大きな穴が開きます。周囲には叔父が運んできたお椀などが散乱し、叔父の遺体もバラバラになっていました。しばらくした。

たってから、飛び散った手足を拾い集め箱に入れて埋葬したそうです。
というのは、そのとき私は壕の横穴にいて、爆風で壕が崩れ生き埋めになってしまったのです。駆けつけてくれた村人たちによって掘り出され、一命は取り留めたものの、三日間ほど意識がなく、壕の隅で寝かされていたそうです。

話は戻りますが、私たち四人はやっと本部富士の壕に到着しました。ところが、そこは兵隊がいっぱいで、母が必死に頼んでも誰も返事もしません。上官らしい男が棒を振り上げ、私たちは追い払われました。

米軍上陸に備えて、村人は家族で壕を掘るのですが、兵隊も自分たち用に掘ります。地形に詳しい村人たちは頑丈な地盤を探して掘るのですが、兵隊はところかまわず掘り、途中で土が柔らかく崩れやすいところだと分かると掘るのをやめ、他の場所を探してまた掘るので、友軍の掘った未完

嘉数廣子

結局、私たちは、そんな未完成の浅い壕に行かざるを得ませんでした。壕と妹たちが殺された墓を往復しているとき、私はマラリアに罹りました。四〇度を超える高熱で体がブルブルと震え、意識は朦朧として動くこともできません。

そんな私を、母は、「何でもいいから口に入れろ！ 食べないと死ぬよ！」と言って、棒で叩くのです。余りの痛さに、私は必死になって芋でも稗でも口に入れました。おかげで体力がついたのでしょう、死なずに済んだのです。

私たちは、しばらくは壕にいました。あるとき、用を足しに壕の外に出ると、数人の米兵の声が聞こえたので、慌ててアダンの茂みに隠れました。山の麓にある避難小屋から、老夫婦が手を取り合ってオロオロと出てきた。突然、米兵のうちの一人が何か叫びながら腰の短剣を抜くと、

146

お爺さんの首に切りつけたのです。首がブラ〜ンと垂れ下がり、噴き出した血を浴びて、切りつけた米兵もみるみる真っ赤に染まりました。
お爺さんを抱えていたお婆さんも、胸のあたりを何度も何度も短剣で突き刺されました。老夫婦は血まみれになって倒れ、やがて動かなくなった。しゃがんでその光景の一部始終を見ていた私は、思わず失禁していました。

それから一カ月ほどたって、沖縄戦は終結。
大きな壕にいた人たちは次々と収容所に送られて行きました。私たちの小さな壕にもアメリカ人の指示で日本人の責任者が来ましたが、「いま収容所を建てているが、避難民でいっぱいで間に合わない。ひとまず自分たちの村に戻っていなさい」と言ったので村に戻ってきました。
村には、空襲で焼けた家が二〜三軒ありましたが、わが家は無事でした。

戻った村人は五〜六十人くらいいましたが、「自分たちは米軍に見捨てられた。後で米兵が来て皆殺しにされる」という噂が広がった。
一方、その頃、村でマラリアが流行。「米軍がマラリア菌を蒔いた」という噂も広まり、私は不安でいっぱいでした。
ある日、母が高熱を出し、体をブルブル震わせ始めました。マラリアでした。続いて祖母もマラリアに罹ってしまったのです。
薬はおろか、体温計さえ無い村です。母は覚悟を決めたように、ブルブル震えながら、「私と婆ちゃんは伝染病だと思うから、近づかないように。あんたたちも気をつけて！」と言うと、祖母と奥の部屋に入り、出て来なくなりました。
最初に母が亡くなり、二〜三日後に祖母も息を引き取りました。火葬場が空襲で焼かれていたので、駆けつけてくれた親類が母と祖母を埋葬。このマラリアの流行で、村人は半分になってしまいました。

148

こうして、私と光子の二人だけが残されました。けれど、家も畑もありました。それに、私は早くから母とともに畑仕事をやっていたので野菜や芋の作り方を覚えており、助かりました。私と妹は力を合わせて畑を耕し、芋をたくさん作って市場で売って生活しました。

今でも、小さい女の子を見ると時々、思い出すのです。波打ち際でキャッキャッと声をあげて遊んでいた、恵子とトシ子を。

死んだ母親に寄り添い、泣き続ける幼子

梶原玲子 さん

かじわら・れいこ 一九三三年(昭和八年)十一月生まれ。沖縄戦当時は十一歳で、父親が校長を務める安和国民学校(名護市)に併設された校長住宅に、両親と兄弟六人で暮らしていた。三原にある母親の実家に避難したあと、有津の父の実家に逃げる。その途中、餓死したらしい母の脇で泣く幼子に出会う。生きることが精いっぱいの状況のなか、助けたくても助けることができなかった。その子の泣き声は深く胸に突き刺さり、今も忘れられない。八十二歳。那覇市在住。

梶原玲子さんの記憶

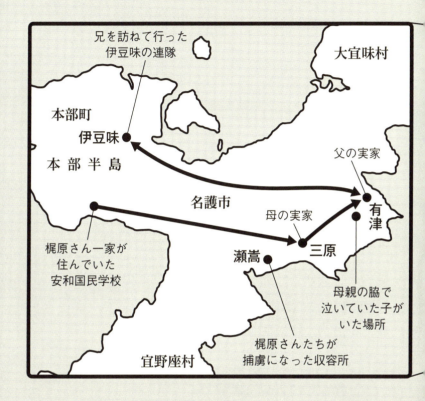

低空飛行で迫る爆撃機の中の米兵の顔がハッキリ見えた

沖縄戦当時、私は国民学校の四年生で十一歳でした。

二年前の昭和十八年に、父が安和(あわ)国民学校の校長に就任したため、両親と長兄（十六歳）、次兄（十三歳）、長女の私、妹（六歳）、弟（三歳）、妹（一歳）の家族八人で名護市安和に引っ越して来ました。

わが家は学校内の校長住宅で、校舎から廊下を渡って行き来できるようになっていましたが、登校する時は一度校門を出て班ごとに集合し、揃(そろ)ったところで六年生を先頭に校門をくぐるという、集団登校でした。

父はとても真面目な人で酒もタバコもやらず、ちょっと融通が利かないところがあって他の教職員の方たちにとっては、煙たい存在だったようです。父は、「過度な貧困は人間を卑屈にさせるが、ある程度、貧しい方が

「人間は清々しく生きられる」という考えの人でした。

私は、上の二人の兄たちと遊んだ記憶はほとんどありません。私は長女だったので、いつも三歳の弟を背負って友達と近くの勝岳に遊びに行ったりしていました。

長兄は、名門の沖縄県立第三中学校に合格。遠くて自宅からは通えないので、父方の祖父母の家に下宿していましたが、すぐに通信兵として十六歳で召集されました。

学校の前には、学年ごとの壕と教職員用の壕、計七つの壕がありました。壕は、三年生以上の生徒たちがグラウンドの周りに掘ったものです。夕コツボのような穴で、見た目は防空壕ですが覆いが無いので上からは丸見えでした。

避難訓練は、突然、笛が「ピー」と鳴ると、「ドン、ドン、ドン」と大

155　梶原玲子

太鼓が打ち鳴らされます。

すると、私たちは何をおいても四年生の自分たちの避難壕へと走るのです。太鼓の音が打ち終わるまでに壕へ駆け込めればいいのですが、間に合わないと太鼓が鳴りやむと同時に、その場に伏せなければなりません。もっとも、履き物もなく、いつも裸足でしたが……。

戦況も厳しくなり、国民学校にもいつの間にか日本兵が入って、校門の前には二人の衛兵がいつも立っていた。三年生以上の生徒は兵隊さんの食料にするためにつわぶきを採りに行きました。

「農業」の科目で使うモッコに、採ってきた大量のつわぶきを入れて前と後ろの二人で担ぎ、学校に運び込みます。そこから先は、割烹着姿（かっぽうぎ）の婦人会の人たちがつわぶきの茎の皮を剥（む）いて干し、保存食にしていました。香

りがあって、ちょっとクセがありますが美味しいのです。

学校には何体もの軍事教練用の藁人形があって、竹やりで藁人形を敵に見立てて突かされた。とくに女子教員は、一人ずつやらされていました。竹の先を斜めに鋭く切り落とし、先に豚の脂を塗り火で炙ると、金属の槍の穂先のような強さになるのです。男の子たちは競って強い竹やりを作っていました。

消火のためのバケツリレーも、今では懐かしく思います。手から手へと渡されたバケツの水を最後の人が火にかけるのですが、コツがあって一気に力を込めてかけないと効果がないと。

また、沖縄では当時、学校で「方言を使ってはいけない」という教育がされていました。うっかり方言を使った子が罰として、横長のノート大の板に「標準語励行」と書かれた札を首から下げさせられていたものです。

梶原玲子

あれは、「一〇・一〇空襲」の前だったと思います。

弟を背負って芋畑を歩いていると、突然、どこからともなく米軍の爆撃機が現れ、低空飛行で私に迫ってきたのです。慌てて芋畑のくぼみに身を寄せ、振り向いたら操縦席の米兵の顔がハッキリと見えました。あの日のことは、その後、何度も思い出され、トラウマになりました。あそこで撃たれたら、私は確実に死んでいたはずです。

そのまま自分たちの壕に戻ると、壕の中でも大騒ぎでした。壕に逃げ込んだ日本兵が、銃を構えて「グラマン機に発砲する」と言うのを、まわりの人たちが、「そんなことをしたら逆にグラマン機から狙い撃ちされる」と、必死で止めていました。

「一〇・一〇空襲」は、学校の離れにあるわが家から見ました。無数の敵

機は司令部のある南部だけでなく、山原(ヤンバル)といわれていた名護・安和の上空にも、爆弾こそ落としませんでしたが、来ていたのです。ゆっくり、ゆっくり飛んでいる敵機に、友軍の爆撃機が応戦していました。

「一〇・一〇空襲」を機に、母は小さな弟妹を連れて、カヌチャ湾の三原にある実家に疎開。

父は学校を守らなくてはいけないということで、私と十三歳の次兄と一緒に残りました。長兄は、十六歳で通信兵として召集され、当時は居所不明になっていた。十三歳の次兄も、その後すぐに学校から通知があり、「鉄血勤皇隊」として召集されました。靴下に、米二合を入れて名護の伊差川(さがわ)に集合して、そこで手榴弾(しゅりゅうだん)二個を渡されたと言います。「いよいよ」と決死の覚悟を決めた頃、「一、二年生は解散!」ということになり、戦場には行かずに済みました。

159　梶原玲子

国民学校は軍に接収されており、校長住宅の隣が兵舎の炊事場になり、朝、昼、夕方にはご飯と味噌汁をバケツに入れて炊事兵が届けてくれました。

 また、校長住宅の離れには新任教師用の八畳間があって、そこに特攻隊の人たちがいつも七～八人いて、よく酒盛りをしていました。といっても、歌を歌ったり、陽気に騒いだりというわけではなく、しんみりと茶碗で酒を酌み交わすといった感じでした。そこから特攻隊の基地に送られていったようです。

 米軍が上陸してくるという噂が入り、とうとう私たちも学校を捨てて母と弟妹たちが疎開している三原の母の実家に避難することになりました。学校では元旦と紀元節には屋内運動場に安置されている木箱に入った天皇陛下のご真影（写真）を拝するのですが、それを箱ごと私が背負い、母

160

の実家に向かいました。母の実家は大農家で、母屋のほかに穀物を貯蔵する大きな納屋がありました。

行ってみると、「一〇・一〇空襲」で焼け出された人たちが何十人と詰めかけていて、母屋から納屋、豚の餌を煮る広い土間まで、屋根のあるところはすべて避難してきた人たちで足の踏み場もありません。しかも、人々は次から次と押し寄せてくるので、納屋の食料もみるみる底を突きました。後から逃げてきた人たちは、「芋の皮でもいいですから、ください」と懇願していました。

私たち家族は、母の実家のある三原から、さらに奥の父の実家である有津(あり)に逃げることになりました。細く曲がりくねっている山道を、避難してきた人たちと一緒に逃げたのです。

有津に着くと、避難してきた人たちの情報で長兄の消息が分かりました。本部町の伊豆味の連隊にいると聞いて、母は、「なんとしても会いに行く！」と言い出したのです。周囲は、「危ないから」と止めましたが、母の気持ちは固く、一歳の妹を私が背負って一緒に行くことになりました。

何日もかけて、私たちはやっと伊豆味の連隊に着きました。ところが、通信兵は各部隊に一人ずつ配属され、長兄は他の部隊に転属になっていて、結局、長兄には会えず、私たちがっかりしながら有津に戻りました。

私たちは有津に二〜三カ月おりました。ある日、長兄がひょっこり姿を現したのです。たまたま撤退して、たどり着いた所が実家のすぐ近くの有銘だったのので、すぐに上官に「面会に行きたい」と話し、上官も「午後二時までに戻るように」と許可してくれたそうです。撤退で一週間余り飲まず食わずで痩せ細った軍服姿の長兄を見て、みんな泣きました。

会えたのもつかの間、戻る時間が迫ってきたので、その日のうちに、土地に詳しい祖父と一緒に戻ることになりました。

その途中、三人の米兵に遭遇したのです。いち早く気づいた祖父が後ろを歩いていた長兄に、「逃げろ！」と合図。祖父は米兵に「年寄りであること」を理由に、何とかごまかして戻って来ました。

結局、長兄は部隊には戻れず、実家の有津に戻って来ました。米兵に会ってからは祖父が、「家にいては危ない。山に隠れよう」と、親類一同、十五人で山奥に隠れました。

この米兵のことは村落の複数の人たちが目撃していたようで、たちまち噂になり、その噂を村にいた数人の日本兵が聞いて、「その米兵を殺そう！」と探しに出かけ、見つけ出して追いかけ、海に飛び込んで岩陰に隠れたところを射殺したそうです。三人とも手を挙げて降伏したのに撃った

163　梶原玲子

そうです。

このことを知った米軍は報復のため、村落全戸に火をかけ焼き払いました。山の上から見ていた私たちは恐ろしくなり、「こうなったら降伏するより仕方ない」と決めたのです。

ところが父、長兄、次兄の三人は、「自分たちは日本兵と間違われて殺される」と考え、その場から逃げ出したのです。

残った十二人は捕虜になり、瀬嵩の収容所に送られました。山奥に逃げ込んだ父たち三人は有銘にたどり着き、そこで運良くハワイ帰りの英語が話せる父の友人に会い、その人から、みんな捕虜になったことを聞き、もう逃げられないと決め、四人で瀬嵩の収容所を目指して歩き始めました。途中、三十人ほどの米兵に遭遇し、父の取り調べ中に、友人が「この人は学校の校長で兵隊ではない」と話し、事なきを得て無事、その場で四人は捕虜になり、ジープに乗せられて瀬嵩の収容所に送られてきました。

私には、どうしても忘れることのできない光景があります。それを思い出すと、今でも胸が痛むのです。

母の実家から、有津の父の実家に逃げる途中、もう少しで有津村落に入るという辺りで突然、赤ん坊の泣き声を聞きました。道がくねっている上に木が生い茂っているので、初めは泣き声しか聞こえませんでした。姿が見えるところまで来ると、道の端に、顔から首、胸元まで真っ黒に日焼けした二十代前半くらいの、母親であろう女性が横わり、その横で両足を投げ出しペタンと座り込んだ男の子がいたのです。

一歳半ぐらいのその子は、まるで火がついたように大声で泣いていました。私たちの一団が通りかかったので泣き出したのかもしれません。

髪はヤマアラシのように伸び放題で、薄汚れたランニングを着ています。気になって立ち止まった私を見上げたその子は、目と口をいっぱいに開け

て、体をよじるように一段と大声で訴えるように泣くのです。
片手で母親のモンペの端をつかんでいるのは、「お母さんを助けて！」と言っているのでしょうか、泣いて訴えているのです。
か。喋れない代わりに、「おなかがすいた」と言っているのでしょうか。
髪は乱れ、ガリガリに痩せた母親に傷らしいものは見当たりません。明らかに餓死でした。荷物らしいものも持っていません。盗られたのか、初めから持っていなかったのか……。
普通、避難する人たちは家族、親類など、集団でいるのに母子だけというのも異様でした。
あの子は、きっと空腹だったと思います。でも、誰も足を止める人はいませんでした。
唯一、私が足を止めたので、顔じゅうを涙で濡らしながら訴えかけたのでしょう。あの瞳を思い出すと、本当にやり切れない思いでいっぱいにな

ります。あの後、あの子はどうなったのでしょう。母親の横で、あのまま餓死したのでしょうか。誰かが連れて行ってくれたのでしょうか。
私も気になって、ちょっとだけ立ち止まりましたが、皆に遅れまいとすぐに歩き出しました。
気になって、何度も何度も振り返ってその子の方を見たけれど、誰もその子の前で立ち止まろうとする人はいませんでした。姿が見えなくなっても、その泣き声だけは、ずっと続いていました。

「対馬丸」で教え子を死なせた母の苦悩

神山洋子 さん

かみやま・ようこ　一九二九年（昭和四年）八月生まれ。沖縄戦当時は沖縄第一高等女学校の三年生。祖母と、地元の小学校教師の母、女子師範学校に通う姉の四人で那覇市垣花に住んでいた。対馬丸の撃沈で亡くなった学童の親らが家に押しかけて、教師の母に抗議。憔悴しきった母を見ていられなかった。「ひめゆり」として作業に携わるも、戦争が激しくなり家族で避難する。家族は収容所に入れられ、母は自ら申し出て、併設の孤児院で孤児の世話をした。八十七歳。那覇市在住。

神山洋子さんの記憶

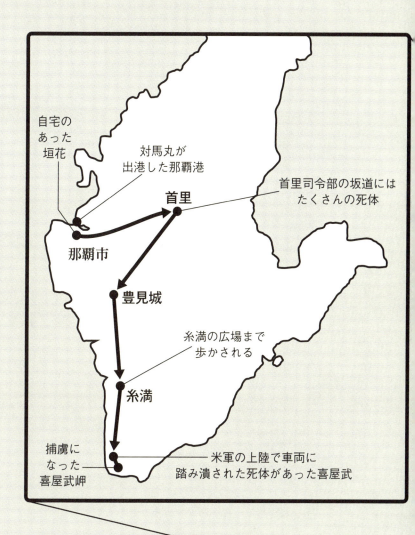

対馬丸が撃沈され、母の教え子の多くが犠牲になった

私の父は、開業医の祖父の一人息子で、沖縄県庁の職員でした。私が二歳のときに父が病気で亡くなったので、父との思い出はほとんどありません。

父亡き後、祖父も亡くなり、沖縄戦の頃は祖母、母と十八歳の姉、私の女四人の生活でした。

母は地元の垣花（かきのはな）国民学校の教師をしており、姉は沖縄県立第一高等女学校から女子師範に進学。私は第一高等女学校の三年生でした。第一高等女学校は明治から続く沖縄の名門女学校で、昔から「ひめゆり」の愛称で呼ばれていました。ちなみに母も「ひめゆり」の出身です。

「ひめゆり」の紺色のセーラー服は地元男子学生の憧れの的でしたが、私

たちのときから戦時中ということで、上はヘチマ襟(えり)のブラウスで下はモンぺという制服になってしまいました。

学校が同じ敷地内にあるので、毎朝、姉と私は旭橋から嘉手納(かでな)線に乗って一緒に通学。地元の小学校教師の母は、私たちを見送った後に出勤します。家事一切は祖母がやっていたので、母は若い先生方に代わって遅くまで学校に残って仕事をしていました。この頃までは穏やかな日常でした。

それがあんな地獄を見ることになろうとは——。

一九四四年（昭和十九年）八月、戦況も厳しくなってきたので、那覇市内八校の小学校の児童約八百人が九州の長崎に疎開することになり、母も引率教師として行くことになりました。

疎開は教員家族も同行できることになり、話し合った末、家族全員で疎開することにしました。

長崎に家屋を一軒借りて、「垣花と同じように生

活しよう」と決めたのです。家財道具も送り、当日、身の回りの物だけ持って対馬丸が出港する那覇港に行きました。

ところが、そこへ、疎開未登録の若い教師夫婦が来て、急遽「代わってほしい」と言うのです。係の人も、「疎開先で児童の世話をするのは若い教師夫婦の方がよい」と言い、私たち家族の疎開は突然、中止になってしまいました。

ところが数日後、その対馬丸がアメリカの潜水艦に撃沈されたことを知らされたのです。当時は戦意高揚のため、すぐにはニュースにならなかったようですが、学校で教師仲間から事実を聞かされた母は、ひどくショックを受けたようです。多くの学童が亡くなり、父母、その他を含め約一千五百人近くが犠牲になったのでした。

しばらくして親たちの知るところとなり、朝早くから夜遅くまで、子どもを亡くした遺族がわが家に押しかけてきました。わが家は地元で祖父が

174

開業医、母も学校教師ということで父母からとても信頼されていたのです。しかも、古くから教師をやっていた母は、問題児などを一手に引き受けていたようで、悪童たちからは、「チューバー（怖い）先生」と呼ばれていました。

突然、わが子を失った親たちは、その怒りや悲しみの持って行き場がないので、うちに来たのだと思います。

「牧志（旧姓）先生が行くというから、うちの子を出したのに、先生は行かずにうちの子だけなぜ！」「沈没する船に、なぜうちの子を乗せたんです！」と、口々に訴えます。

母も、抗議する親に会うと、一人ひとりの教え子の顔を思い出すらしく、ただ、ただ「○○君、ごめんなさい！」「○○ちゃん、許して！」と、畳に手をついて頭を下げる毎日でした。

また、母は学校へ行くと、遺族に責められて意気消沈している若い教師

175　神山洋子

たちを励ましていたそうです。
そんな母も遺族が帰り、一人になると、「なぜ私だけ生き残ってしまったのだろう。この先、のうのうと生きてなどいられない！」と、生き残った罪悪感で、深夜まで考え込んでいました。それは、見ていられないほどでした。

一方、「ひめゆり」では、全校生徒が、「兵隊さんの手伝い」に駆り出されていました。
私たちは、小禄（おろく）飛行場に砲台を築く作業に従事。「作業袋」という布袋に土を詰めて運んだり、二人一組で土を入れたカマス（藁（わら）ムシロでできた袋）を担いだりしました。
また、怪我（けが）などの応急処置を学校で教わったので、作業中に怪我をした同級生や兵隊のために、消毒薬をつけたり包帯を巻いたりしました。

映画などで有名な「従軍看護生」の「ひめゆり学徒隊」というのは、戦時中、特に戦が激しくなってきたときに、早朝の集合や夜遅くまでの団体行動が可能な寄宿舎の生徒たちで、急遽、結成された組織です。第一高女の中でも離島や山原など遠方の地域の女学生たちで、那覇市内や私たちのような汽車通学生は入っていません。

私は寄宿舎生ではなかったので、特に親しい人はいませんでしたが、同期で亡くなった方々はほとんど知っています。一、二年生のときに一緒だった人など、大勢いました。

戦後、落ち着いてから、同期会に出席した通学生の私たちは、亡くなった寄宿舎生一人ひとりの名前を挙げて、その方々を偲んだものです。

やがて空襲が激しくなり、私たち家族は垣花から避難することになりました。司令部のある首里に行けば兵隊もたくさんいて、守ってもらえるだ

ろうと、祖母、母、姉、私の四人で出発。

ところが、首里に着いて唖然(あぜん)としました。死体が転がっているのです。それも全員、女、子どもです。司令部に向かう坂道いっぱいに、死体がすべて、防衛隊として徴用されていたので、誰もいません。友軍の兵隊も、どこへ行ったのか一人も見えませんでした。

死体は海上からの艦砲射撃と、上空からの爆撃で殺された人たちでした。しかも、首里司令部が陥落し、上陸した米軍の戦車が何台もそれらの死体の上を通過したため、死体はすべて、ボロ雑巾(ぞうきん)のようにちぎれたり、骨が砕けたりして衣類と皮だけになっていたのです。何台もの戦車やトラックが通過したので、血はどこにも残っていないのです。

最初の一台目に轢(ひ)かれたときは出血したでしょうが、何台も通過するうちに車両のキャタビラやタイヤが、死体の血を吸い取っていったのです。そみんな、私たち家族のように司令部を頼りに逃げてきた人たちです。そ

の無数の死体を見たとたん、母に背負われるようにしていた祖母がシャンとなりました。これまで、医者の奥さんとして、どこへ行くにも人力車なしでは移動したことのなかった祖母が、自分の足でサッサと歩くようになったのです。

全滅の首里から、私たちは島尻の喜屋武岬を目指して逃げることにしました。なぜ、山原の方に逃げなかったかというと、本部に祖父の牧志医院の分院があって、夏になると海水浴を兼ねて家族で、よくバスで行ったものですが、朝出発しても到着は夜になるほど、不便なところなのです。そんなところに徒歩で、しかも祖母を連れては、たどり着くのは無理と判断したのです。

豊見城を通って糸満の喜屋武岬まで、食料係は私が担当しました。私は丈夫で、体力があったからです。母は祖母の面倒を見なければならず、姉

は肺を患っていたので歩くのがやっとでした。

　爆撃で住民は逃げ、あちこちで家屋が燃えています。焼け残った家に入ると、大抵、食料保存用のカメがあり、持ち出せなかった芋や豆がまだ残っていました。土間などに散乱している鍋や釜に、その芋や豆を入れて燻（くすぶ）っている焼け跡に置くと、たちまち焼き芋や焼き豆ができました。夜になると、住民が逃げてしまって空いた壕（ごう）を探して家族で入りました。

　やっと喜屋武岬までたどり着くと、そこも首里と同じ光景が広がっていました。すでに米軍の上陸が始まっていて、たくさんの車両が移動しています。軍用トラックや戦車などに轢（ひ）き潰（つぶ）された女、子どもの死体が、ボロ雑巾のように皮状になって無数に転がっていました。女、子どもなので骨格がしっかりしていない分、潰されやすいのでしょうか。もちろん血もな

いし、乾燥しているのかハエもたかっていません。いくら戦時中だからといって、死体も片付けずに、その上を軍用トラックで踏み潰していくなんて……。

その夜、私たち家族は小さな壕を探して休みました。翌朝、壕を出てみると、突然、何台ものジープがやってきて次々と米兵が降りて来ました。すでに、いくつかの壕に避難民がいることが分かっていたようです。その まま、私たちは他の避難民と一緒に糸満の広場まで歩かされました。

広場にはたくさんの避難民がいました。数日、その広場で過ごした後、各収容所行きのトラックに乗せられ、私たちは石川の収容所に入れられた。収容所に到着したとたん、母が「牧志先生！」と、疎開しなかった児童の一人から声をかけられ、母の顔はみるみる歪み、いまにも泣き出しそうになりました。対馬丸で教え子を死なせてしまったという辛い思いが、再び戻って来たのです。

その場で、母は「収容所の孤児院で子どもたちの世話をしたい」と係官に申し出ました。収容所には、戦争で親を亡くした孤児がたくさん収容されていたのです。どの収容所にも、孤児院がありました。
母が孤児院に行ったので、私たちは石川の収容所を出るまで、母とは別々の生活を送っていました。

ひめゆり学徒隊として負傷兵を看護

新川初子 さん

あらかわ・はつこ　一九二六年（昭和元年）五月生まれ。沖縄戦当時は十九歳で、沖縄女子師範学校本科二年生だった。看護訓練を受け、「ひめゆり学徒隊」のメンバーとなる。南風原陸軍病院壕で負傷兵の看護や「飯上げ」に従事。迫撃砲弾の破片が足首に突き刺さり、大怪我を負う。陸軍病院が移動することになり、動けない者には青酸カリが配られた。下級生に支えられながら逃げ、やがて皆と手榴弾での自決を決意。米兵に発見され、真喜屋の病院に連行された。九十歳。大阪・豊中市在住。

新川初子さんの記憶

怪我で横たわる枕元に青酸カリが置かれた

　終戦になって、「ひめゆり学徒隊」の半数以上が亡くなったことを知ったときは、ただただ、亡くなった学友に申し訳なくて、「私は逃げて生き延びた」という罪悪感で長い間苦しみました。

　私は京都出身で、警察官だった父が京都府警勤務から実家のある沖縄に転勤したため、京都府立桃山高等女学校から沖縄県立第一高等女学校三年に編入しました。

　一九四三年（昭和十八年）、沖縄師範学校本科に進学。沖縄師範学校女子部と第一高等女学校は同じ敷地内にある併地校で、第一高女を卒業して師範女子に進学する人が多かったと思います。女学校から「師範学校予科」に行かず、い私は寄宿舎生になりました。

きなり本科に入った女学生は寄宿舎入居が義務づけられていたからです。女学校出はよく笑うしお喋りをするので、今の「自由奔放」という意味の「自由骨頂」と、よく言われたものです。

翌年、沖縄守備三十二軍が創設され、日本軍が沖縄に駐留。沖縄の人たちに総動員体制が敷かれ、学校の授業も軍の作業にとって代わられた。

米軍上陸に備えて看護訓練が行われました。午後から講堂で、下士官や衛生兵によって、師範女子は二年生、第一高女は三～四年生の上級生が介護訓練を受けました。

また、兵隊さんと一緒に小禄の飛行場造りにも通いました。同級生たちとツルハシを振って硬い珊瑚礁の岩を砕き、ザルに入れて窪地に運び、デコボコの地面を平らな滑走路にするのです。

その飛行場も、米軍上陸で日本軍が一度も使用することなく終わりました。

一九四五年（昭和二十年）三月二十三日、沖縄本島にも米軍の空襲が始まり、翌日、私たち寄宿舎生にも動員命令が出ました。

三月二十三日、師範女子と第一高女の寄宿舎生二二二人と教員一八人。計二四〇人が「ひめゆり学徒隊」として結成された。

三月二十四日、早朝の四時頃でした。寄宿舎生全員が運動場に集められ、校長先生から「皇国の女学生としてしっかりやってもらいたい！」という訓示を受け、「夜の明けきらないうちに到着せよ」と言われました。
私たちは那覇の師範学校から南風原の陸軍病院壕まで歩きました。

三月二十五日に行われるはずだった卒業式は二十九日に延期になり、時折、近くに艦砲が着弾して足元が揺れる中、三角兵舎テントの中でロウソクの薄明かりのもと、行われました。

いままでの師範女子の卒業式には沖縄県知事をはじめ、そうそうたる名士が参列していましたが、私たちのときは民間人では島尻の村長が一人、あとは軍の上官が数人という卒業式でした。卒業証書も、教員免状もありませんでした。

動員先の南風原陸軍病院壕は、「陸軍病院」といっても上空、海上から地表の建物はすべて標的となるので、南風原の山に三十数本もの横穴を掘り、そこを「病院」としていました。

最初、私たちが入った頃は傷病者も少なく、南風原村の避難した民家の

戸板を外して地べたに敷き、病床代わりにしていました。
ところが米軍上陸と共に傷病者が増え、病床として丸太を組んだ二段ベッドがズラリと並ぶことになりました。
当初は外科、内科、伝染病壕と三つに分かれていましたが、四月一日の米軍上陸と共に前線から負傷兵がどんどん送られてくるようになり、第一外科、第二外科、第三外科と、すべて外科に変わりました。砲弾の負傷による外科治療ばかりになったのです。
私は第一外科二十四号壕（三十数号まであった）に下級生二人と同級生二人の四人で配属されました。
下級生はまだ十五歳、重い死体運びや危険な「飯上げ」をさせるのはかわいそうなので、それらは私と同級生が担当しました。狭い穴の中の通路は、人がすれ違うのもやっとでした。
負傷した兵士が亡くなると、頭と足を持って担架に乗せ、壕の外に運び

出します。大柄な兵士の場合、運び出すのが大変でした。

「飯上げ」がなぜ危険かというと、野戦病院（壕）の炊事場は小高い山を二つ越えた喜屋武（きゃん）という所にあったので、砲弾が飛び交う中、木桶（きおけ）に入った兵隊の飯と汁を持って行き来するのは命がけだったのです。

それだけに、他の壕では「飯上げ」は兵隊の任務でしたが、二十四号壕では私たち学徒が担当しました。学徒ということで、よく順番を早めてくれました。

梅雨に入ると山の斜面はぬかるみとなり、ツルツル滑ります。怪我（けが）のため食事がとりにくくなった兵隊用の、お粥（かゆ）の入った飯盒（はんごう）と汁桶（しるおけ）を、こぼすまいと必死で運びました。

その上、暗がりの山道なのでさらに歩きにくいのです。夜七時過ぎの夕食時になると米軍はほとんど撃ってこなくなるので、「飯上げ」はその頃

を見計らって行くことになります。
　ところが、各病院壕からも一斉にやって来るので、百人以上の当番兵が食事桶を持って待つことになるのです。
　七時に出発しても、壕に戻ってくるのは九時頃になります。持ち帰ると、二段ベッドのあちこちから手が伸びて、「早くくれ！」と。その手を払い除け、壕の奥へ入るのでした。
　米軍からは、完全に病院壕は見つかっていたと思います。その証拠に、横殴りの雨のように絶え間なく、ビュンビュンと機銃の弾丸は飛んで来るし、時折、ドーンと艦砲が着弾するのです。
　すると、直径五〜六メートルの穴が開き、近くにいた人は木端微塵です。周囲には飛び散った土砂の山ができました。
　艦砲は破壊力が強いので、その合間を縫って飛び出すのですが、機銃の

弾丸に当たることがあります。機銃の弾丸はほとんどが体を貫通し、弾丸が入ったところは焼いた火箸を突き刺した程度の穴ですが、抜ける部分は「肉の花」といって、花が咲いたように肉塊が大きく飛び出します。
壕の中は糞尿、汗、血膿で息をするのも辛いほどの臭気でした。そこで、少しでも外の空気を吸おうと入り口の方に出て、撃たれる学徒が何人もいました。
壕の中は、「軍医殿！」「助けてくれ！」「便器を！」「尿器を！」の怒号が飛び交います。「おっかあ！」などの悲鳴と、収容されているのは、目を覆うばかりの重症患者ばかり。重症患者の便や尿をとるのも、私たちの仕事の一つでした。
動員されたときは、最多で四〜五人だった傷病者が、百十八人にものぼるようになりました。

傷口にはたちまち銀蠅が飛んできて、みるみる白い蛆虫がたかります。米粒のような小さな蛆虫が上になったり下になったりして山盛りになると、一匹の大きさが小指の先ほどに太っているのです。

背中全面を負傷した兵隊は、寝返りを打つこともできず這いつくばったままでした。その背中一面に白い蛆虫が蠢いているのです。

その蛆虫が、「プチャプチャ」と傷口を食む音が聞こえました。最初は、一つ一つピンセットで摘まんで捕っていましたが、埒があかないので上着の裾を広げ、掻き寄せるようにして壕の外に捨てに行きました。

ところが、蛆虫は、「蛆虫治療」といわれるほど、傷口の膿をきれいに食べるので傷痕がツルツルになるのです。

大変なのは、銀蠅が耳の穴に卵を産み付けたときでした。突然、「耳の中が痛い」と、のたうち回り、喚き出す人がいるのですが、耳の穴の中なのでどうすることもできないのです。

194

傷病者が多くなると、三日に一回の包帯交換が五日に一度、一週間に一度になります。血液は鉄分を多く含んでいるので固まると鉄のように硬く重くなり、なかなか剥がれません。

「もっとやさしくやれよ！」と怒鳴られるのですが負傷兵は大勢いるし、一人に時間を掛けていられないのです。

血膿で固まった包帯を、腐った皮膚ごと剥がすと「ゴトン」と鉄の塊を落としたような音をたてました。

頭をやられた兵隊は、「脳症」といって、正常な自覚がなくなり、隣の兵隊の傷口や顔を踏んだり、ベッドの下の兵隊の顔にオシッコをしたりします。

そのたびに、「何とかしてくれ！」と怒鳴られました。昼夜のない忙しさのためか、横になって寝たりトイレに行った記憶すらありません。

みんな気が立っていました。

だから、「はい」「ちょっと待ってください」「スミマセン」。朝から晩まで、この言葉以外、口にできませんでした。

それでも、「沖縄の女子学生は情がない」「飯上げに行って、自分たちだけ食べている」などと罵られ、辛い思いをしました。

負傷兵が増えるにつれて、壕を奥へ奥へと掘り進めるので、私たちは足りなくなったベッドを作る丸太の切り出しまでやりました。

五月十三日、私は「飯上げ」に行き、空井戸の陰で順番を待っていました。

数日前に私の履いていた地下足袋を見て、兵隊さんが「そんなんじゃ砲弾が飛んできたらひとたまりもないぞ」と、革製の軍靴を貸してくれまし

た。鉄の鋲が何本も打ってあるので、歩くと重かったです。
このときは、艦砲ではなくて迫撃砲弾でした。迫撃砲は、着弾すると破片がいくつも飛び散ります。
一瞬、何が起こったか分からなかったけれど、後で聞くと七センチ四方の真っ赤に焼けた迫撃砲の破片が、私の左足のくるぶしに突き刺さって止まったのでした。軍靴をはいてなかったら、左足はなかったと思います。
余談ですが、迫撃砲の破片は木に当たるとスパッと切り倒すほどの威力があります。ところが、蘇鉄だけは、シュッと刺さると突き抜けずそのまま止まるのです。これは、蘇鉄の特性なのかもしれません。
砲弾での怪我は、火薬の成分が血管を通って脳に届き、脳症を起こします。こうなると、自分で自分が分からなくなるのです。沖縄戦では、砲弾の火薬で脳症を起こした兵隊がたくさんいました。

だから、私も傷口だけでなく周囲の皮膚もピンセットでつまんで、麻酔もかけずハサミでジョキジョキと大きく切られました。
日頃、手足を切断されて苦しくて「殺してくれ！」などと叫ぶ兵隊さんに、「皇国の軍人でしょう！」などと言っていた手前、私は悲鳴を上げるわけにはいきません。
軍医が、「ほう、女学生の方が並みの兵隊より強いな」と褒めてくれましたが、麻酔も無い中での手術は激痛で声も出なかったのです。
また、消毒薬のヨードチンキは猛者の兵隊でも悲鳴をあげるほど痛く、焼けた火箸を当てられたような痛みが脳天を突き抜けました。
当時、軍が使っていた消毒薬のヨードチンキは薄めない、真っ黒な原液でした。というのは、壕の中は不潔で、傷口から破傷風を引き起こすため、それを防ぐには原液が必要だったのです。
第一外科二十四号壕の一番奥の狭い隙間(すきま)に体を入れて、私は十日ほど横

ある日、何だか壕の中の空気に異常を感じました。同級生が顔を出して、「初ちゃん、ここに置いとくよ。すぐに連れに来るからね」と言って、頭の上の方に何かを置いて立ち去りました。
間もなく、二段ベッドから「バタン」、「バタン」と何かが倒れる音、手榴弾の爆発する音、「連れて行ってください！」という悲痛な叫び声が聞こえました。
実はこのとき、首里の三十二軍司令部は陥落寸前。軍は本土決戦を先延ばしさせるため司令部の南部撤退を選択し、南風原の陸軍病院壕は閉鎖されることになったのです。
この日は、ちょうど私の十九歳の誕生日でした。

行先は、島尻の陸軍病院本部の山城の壕に。第一外科と第三外科は、後に「ひめゆりの塔」が建てられた伊原（いはら）の壕、第二外科は糸洲の壕に移ることになった。

何とか歩ける「独歩患者」は連れて行き、歩けない患者には青酸カリを入れた牛乳や自決用の手榴弾が配られました。
「バタン」「バタン」と倒れる音は、青酸カリを含んで死亡し、ベッドから落ちる音でした。絶望して手榴弾で自決する者、這（は）いずりながら「連れて行ってくれ！」と泣き叫ぶ者が大勢いたように思います。
私は、ただならぬ壕の中の雰囲気は感じるものの、それが何であるかは知らされていませんでした。

そこへ突然、二人の下級生が飛び込んで来て「早く行きましょう！」

「初子姉さん行きましょう！」とせき立てるのです。
「どこへ行くの？」「もう、なんでもいいから早く、そうでないと大変なんです。早く早く」と。

壕のすぐ近くまで、米軍は迫っていました。

砲弾が炸裂する中を下級生に支えられて、たどり着いたら、そこには担架が三つあり、すでに二つには重症の学徒が横たわっていました。

残った担架は学校の教師が乗るはずだったのですが、脳症がひどくなり、暴れて連れ出すのが困難だったそうです。そこで、先生が下級生たちに「仲村（私の旧姓）を連れて来い」と指示されたのでした。

そうでなかったら、私は壕の中で薬だと思って青酸カリを飲んで死んでいたはずです。

私は、そうとは知りませんでしたが、枕元には米、牛乳、それに、紙に包んだ粉薬のような青酸カリが置かれていたからです。

砲弾の嵐の中を、担架に乗って南部へ逃げました。

「四～五人でいいですから、入れてください」と、あちこちの壕で交渉するのですが、どこの壕も兵隊でいっぱいでした。ときには日本刀で脅かされたこともありました。

担架を担いだ防衛隊員が艦砲で負傷すると、学徒が交代で運んでくれました。

私の怪我は片足だけでしたが、皆のようには歩けません。迷惑をかけているのが辛かったです。

こうして、やっと南部の伊原の壕にたどり着きました。

それもつかの間、六月十八日、学徒隊に突然、「解散命令」が出ました。

上官から、「君たちはもう用が無くなった。自由行動をとれ！」と言わ

202

れたのです。私たちは一人でも多くいた方が心強いと思いましたが、そうすると目立ちます。

先生は「なるべく四～五人ずつ固まって敵中を突破しなさい。命だけは大切に」と言いました。

そして、「絶対に捕虜にだけはなるな！」と、悲痛な声で叫びました。いずれにしても、弾丸に当たって死ぬか自決しか道はなかったのです。

「ひめゆり学徒隊」の死亡者は教師一三人、女学生一二三人。その中で「突然の解散命令」で一〇〇人以上が解散の数日後、自決で亡くなっている。

砲弾が飛んでくる戦場で「自由にしろ！」と言われても、どこへ行ったらいいのか分かるはずもありません。

陸中突破は、敵兵だらけなので無理です。海岸線を行くしかありませんでした。

名城・糸満の西海岸は砂浜で隠れるところがないので、私たちは岩や絶壁の多い摩文仁(まぶに)の東海岸を目指すことにしました。

昼間は岩陰に隠れて、夜になったら歩き出します。

その頃になると、私は杖につかまりながら何とか歩けるまでに回復していました。時折、砲弾が飛んで来る暗闇の中を、友達の姿を見失うまいと必死でした。

たくさんの死体を跨(また)ぎ、海岸までたどり着いたときは、すでに靴も破れて裸足でした。珊瑚礁の表面は針のように鋭く、たちまち足の裏はズル剝(む)けになりました。

一歩進むごとに、胸の芯(しん)まで痛みが走ります。特に、焼けた砂の上は、

まるで炭火の上を歩いているようでした。それでも米兵に気づかれるといけないので、悲鳴すらあげられません。自分一人が捕虜になりでもしたら、みんなに迷惑がかかります。その思いだけで、無言で歩き続けました。

摩文仁の海岸に出ましたが、周囲の海は米艦で埋め尽くされていました。私は、「もうこれ以上は逃げられない！」と覚悟を決めました。皆の気持ちも一緒でした。「捕まって辱めを受けるより自決しよう！」と決めたのです。

不思議と気持ちは落ち着いていました。一緒に行動してきた七～八人が車座になりました。手榴弾の安全ピンを抜き、地面に叩き付けたのと同時に、われ先に手榴弾の上に覆いかぶさりました。

櫛で髪を梳かす者、家族の写真を眺めて別れを惜しむ者、救急袋から制服を取り出して着替える者、それぞれが死出の準備をしました。

205　新川初子

皆、一番下になって木端微塵に死にたい、との思いからです。手足だけの怪我で生き残ったら「ハワイの慰安所」に送られる。そう信じていたのです。

けれど、持っていた手榴弾は二個とも不発でした。

途方にくれていると、突然、岩陰から銃を持った米兵が三～四人現れました。十二歳ぐらいの沖縄の少年が一緒でした。

「姉さんたち、戦争は終わったよ」と少年が言いましたが、「あんたは米軍のスパイだろう！ 同じ日本人にどうして嘘を言うの！」と、私たちは言い返しました。

日本人同士のそんなやり取りには構わず、米兵は銃を突きつけ追い立てます。連行されたところは摩文仁の広場でした。

そこには大勢の避難民がいました。私たちは一列になって、トラックま

で歩かされました。
その途中で、上半身裸の米兵が、列の中から何人かをピックアップしていました。集められた私たちは全員、学徒でした。
トラックに乗せられて、着いたのは真喜屋の病院でした。米兵は学徒が負傷者の看護ができることを、すでに知っていたようです。
連行されながら下級生と手を繋ぎ、「太平洋の真ん中に行ったら甲板から飛び込んで死のうね」とささやきましたが、私たちがハワイに送られることはありませんでした。

覚悟を決めて集団死の現場へ

田中美江 さん

たなか・みえ　一九三〇年（昭和五年）十月生まれ。沖縄戦当時、座間味島の阿佐村落に祖母と母、兄弟三人で暮らしていた。座間味島の大空襲で村は焼け落ち、壕に避難したが、米軍が上陸すると国民学校の先生に促され、集団死を決意。しかし、手榴弾が爆発せず、怖くなって自然洞窟の壕に逃げる。そこに避難してきた人々は、目撃した集団死の様子を語った。母は命がけで日本軍の倉庫から食料を持ち出し、家族を守った。八十五歳。座間味島在住。

田中美江さんの記憶

「そろそろ自決しましょう！」と言われ、
「はい！」と答えた

　座間味島の阿佐にあった大きなわが家は、沖縄特産のアイゴの稚魚・スクガラスの塩辛の製造で成功した祖父が建てました。
　わが家は裕福で、子どもの頃、雨が降って外で遊べないときは、部屋がたくさんある家の中で、弟や妹とかくれんぼをして遊んだものです。座間味でもひときわ大きな家だったので、戦時中は上官の宿舎になったこともあります。
　父は連絡艇を持っていて、その機関長でした。けれど、私が小学二年生（昭和十三年）のときに、支那事変（日中戦争）で戦死。座間味島の最初の戦死者でした。
　このときの戦争（日中戦争）は勝ち戦だったので、母は九州・鹿児島まで

遺骨を引き取りに行き、お葬式には隣の阿嘉島からも多くの人が参列。後に、マカーの忠魂碑に父の名前が刻まれ、その忠魂碑の叙幕引きは私が行いました。

父が亡くなったので、わが家は祖母、母、私、妹、弟の五人家族になりました。

祖母は、大のきれい好きで、床も廊下もピカピカに磨き、子どもが裸足で歩くと足跡が付くというので、私たちはよく叱られました。

そんな祖母に仕えていた母は、とても働き者で、父が亡くなった後も、家で取れた野菜を漬物にして品評会に出品し、一位になるほどで、休んでいるところを見たことがありません。

母は夜明けとともに浜に行き、イザリ（潮干狩り）でタコや魚を取ってきて、私たちが起きてくる頃には、台所のザルに上げてありました。

田中美江

当時、学校の弁当は芋が当たり前で、ご飯を持ってくる子どもは珍しいほどでした。給食は週に一度、ユシ豆腐（硬い島豆腐になる前の軟らかい豆腐）が出て、これが楽しみでした。

運動靴や衣類が切符制だったので、靴がなくて裸足で学校に来る子どもいました。戦争が激しくなると、校庭の二宮金次郎の銅像も供出のためなくなってしまいました。

沖縄戦当時、私は座間味国民学校高等科二年生。一九四四年（昭和十九年）に入ってすぐの頃から、校舎は友軍が使用しました。それでいて、友軍が使った便所の汲み取りは生徒がやらされていました。

三月二十三日は、座間味島への大空襲がありました。その日は、マチャン（真喜武）山の開墾に行く日で、そこに芋を植える予定でした。全校生徒が集まり、阿佐村落のンチャーラ浜を並んで歩き山に到着。

214

ンチャーラ浜のアダンの茂みには、特攻隊の突貫ボート（特攻艇）が隠してあり、兵隊がいつも監視していました。ここを通るときは、たとえ畑に行くのでも証明書の提出を求められた。

ところが、山に着くか着かないうちに、突然、グラマン機の大編隊が飛んできて、たちまち緑の山一面が火の海となったのです。生徒は泣き叫んで逃げ惑い、先生方も右往左往で、ともかくンチャーラ浜に降りて、家に急ぎました。この空襲で、マチャン山から座間味の山々が三日間、燃え続けた。

浜に降りると、阿佐の阿護の浦で爆撃に遭い、船体のあちこちが爆弾の焼け跡だらけのカツオ船がありました。その船に乗っていた漁師二人は直撃弾で即死し、船長は大怪我を負いました。

先生方が学校に戻ったときは、すでに学校は焼け落ちて、形さえなかっ

たそうです。
　私の住んでいた阿佐村落でも家が二軒焼け落ち、弟は爆風で吹き飛ばされ、あわてて赤崎（岳）の麓のユヒナの壕に逃げ込みました。どこの壕も避難民でいっぱいでした。
　空襲は三日間続き、二十六日に米軍が上陸。九時から予定されていた座間味国民学校の卒業式は中止になりました。
　座間味島には、私たちの阿佐村落、学校や郵便局がある座間味村、そして島の西側の阿真村落という三つの村がありました。
　座間味村落は爆撃でメチャクチャになりました。私たち家族は弟が入っているユヒナの壕に避難。ここは、百人ぐらいが入れる大きな洞窟で、学校の先生や父母、生徒なども避難していました。
　米軍上陸当日、ユヒナの壕に集まっていた人たちに、阿佐村落担当の上

原先生が、「座間味村では役場の職員が村民に『自決しますのでマカーの忠魂碑のところに集まるように』と一軒一軒回っている」と話しました。
「こちらも、そろそろ自決しましょう!」と言われたので、私は「はい!」と返事をして、一歳年上のいとこのアイちゃんと上原先生のところに行きました。

母と妹もいましたが、母は目を大きく見開き、恐怖で青ざめた顔をしていました。妹はベソをかき、今にも泣き出しそうです。でも止めることもできず黙って見ているだけでした。

私は悲しくなって、妹に「さようなら」と言うと急に怖くなり、立っていられないほどでした。後のことはハッキリ覚えていません。上原先生の周りに十二、三人の生徒や父母が集まっていました。

やがて、先生が思い切り、手榴弾を床に打ち付けたのです。でも、爆発

はしませんでした。手榴弾が爆発しなかったので、上原先生はカミソリを出してきて研ぎ始めたのです。私は怖くなり、ヌンルルーガマに逃げました。

ヌンルルーガマは大きな自然洞窟で、何百人も入れるし、出入り口があちこちにあってどこからでも出入りできました。島の人たちは誰に指示されたわけでもないのに、最後は大きなヌンルルーガマに逃げようと決めていたようで、すごい人数でした。

ヌンルルーガマでは、逃げてきた人たちが島内の自決の様子を語り合っていました。

「座間味村のマカーでは皆が集まったが、『家族がバラバラでは死ねない』と、家族を探しに行き、自決がウヤムヤになった」とか、「産業組合の壕ではすでに自決が始まり、六十八人が死亡した」などという話でした。

218

「産業組合の壕」というのは、座間味村の役場や郵便局、組合などの職員とその家族が入れる壕で、他の島民が自決に行って追い返されたといいます。

この壕では、家族全員がお正月用の晴れ着を着て、一人ひとりキチンと並んで眠るように死んでいたそうです。六十八人もの人々が整然と並べた亡くなっていたので、「数人の代表格の人が、一人ずつ殺して整然と並べた後、自分たちも自決したのでは」と言われていました。

「教職員の壕では、校長先生夫妻、内間とし子先生、島の女性がいて、初めに手榴弾の爆発で内間先生と島の女性が即死。校長先生は、カミソリで奥さんの首を切り、次に自分の首も切って即死した。ところが、奥さんの首の傷は浅かったので死に切れず、生き返った」という話も聞きました。

戦後、しばらくは、校長先生の奥さんを見かけることもありましたが、

その後、息子さんたちに引き取られて、島を去られたようです。

近所に住む宮平邦夫君の家族は、お父さんがカミソリで最初に邦夫君の首を切り、次に奥さんの首も切ったのですが、これも傷が浅かったのか、奥さんは死に切れなかったのです。

戦後、奥さんはいつも首に布を巻いていましたが、話をするとき空気が漏れたような感じで、聞きとりにくかったことを覚えています。邦夫君のお父さんも、自分では死に切れずに生き残りました。

また、「郵便局のある山の麓の壕では、手榴弾やカミソリがないため、二家族が首を絞め合って自決した。幼い子どもたちも全員、絞殺されていた。手榴弾やカミソリのように一瞬で死ねないので、亡くなっている様子は凄惨だった」という話も耳にしました。

阿真村落の墓に避難した人たちもいましたが、爆撃で墓が破壊され、生き埋めになって亡くなってしまいました。

爆撃といえば、近くのヤギ小屋では、兵隊と島の青年たち十人ぐらいが爆撃で死亡。三月二十六日の米軍上陸が始まってからは、残った日本兵は山へ逃げてしまい、村落に兵隊は一人もいませんでした。

ヌンルルーガマには母と妹も避難してきたものの、食べ物がないので、母は二〜三人の人を誘ってヤマトンマ（大和馬）と呼ばれていた日本軍の倉庫（壕）に米を盗みに行きました。ヤマトンマは海に近いため、潮が引かないと行かれません。海が荒れたときの、マグロ船などの避難場所になっていた所です。

母の話では、壕の中には自決した兵隊の死体が大量にあって、入り口を塞（ふさ）いでいたと。壕の中は暗く、手探りで米俵の積んであるところを探し出しましたが、そこにも十五〜十六人の死体が米俵の上に折り重なっていました。どかそうとして足をかけると、腐っているため、死体のおなかに足

221　田中美江

首までが埋まったそうです。
　ともかく死体をどけて、米を持ち帰った母たちは真夜中、ンチャーラ浜のアダンの下で炊き出しをしました。
　ヌンルルーガマにはクラガー（地下水）もなく、海水が流れ込んでくるので炊事ができません。ンチャーラ浜の近くには田んぼの灌漑用の溜まり水の池があって、それを飲み水や炊事に使ったり、体を洗ったり、洗濯にも使っていました。
　母たちが炊き出しをしたので、ガマにいた人たちもヤマトンマに米を取りに押しかけました。浜には、次第に炊き出しの人たちが増えてきました。久米兵は、夜は動かないので、みんな安心して炊き出しができました。しぶりのご飯は、すごく美味しかったです。

ユヒナの壕の入り口には、婦人会が栽培していた大根やニンジンが植えてあったので、それを抜いてきておかず代わりに生でかじりました。ガマには、産気づいた娘さんがいて、家族が心配そうに付き添っていましたが、数日後、いよいよ生まれるということになって、おばあちゃんとお母さんがアダンの茂みにその娘を連れて行き出産しました。あのお産は、大変だったと思います。

その頃になると、米軍の飛行機からしょっちゅうビラが撒かれました。

「戦争は終わった。安心して出てきなさい」という内容でした。

阿佐村落の上原区長が、「捕虜になっても殺されたりはしません。皆さん、大丈夫ですから出ていきましょう」と言ったのを、どこからか日本兵が聞きつけ、上原区長が家に物を取りに戻ったところ、待ち構えていた兵に射殺されました。

その後、私たち家族は、叔父叔母の家族と一緒に十人以上で、ヌンルルーガマとユヒナガマの中間に大きな穴を見つけて入りました。昼は様子を見に赤崎に登り、夜は穴に戻って寝ました。山の中には、至るところに爆撃で殺された日本兵の腐った死体が転がっていました。島は米軍に制圧されており、阿護の海では米兵たちが遊び半分にランチボートを乗り回し、湾内から島の様子を監視していました。
ある日、母がランチボートの米兵に見つかってしまい、あわてて穴に戻りましたが、ボートから米軍本部に連絡したのか、あっという間に数台のジープが穴の前にやってきて、全員捕虜になってしまいました。
男たちは座間味村の米軍本部に連れて行かれ、島民か兵隊かを徹底的に調べられ、兵隊だと分かるとハワイまで連行。女、子どもは阿真村落で降ろされました。

何日かたって、阿真村落の人たちは村に残され、阿佐村落の人たちは自分たちの村落に戻されました。

その頃から、山に隠れている日本兵に手を焼いた米軍によって阿佐のンチャーラ浜には地雷が埋められました。というのは、古座間味には米軍のゴミ捨て場が設けられていて、鍋、釜から、まだ食べられそうなハム、ソーセージまで、何でも捨ててありました。物資のない頃なので、島民はそれらを自由に拾っていいことになっていたのです。「古座間味の米軍ゴミ捨て場に食べ物がある」ということは、山に隠れていた日本兵も知っていました。

けれど、浜に地雷が埋めてあることは住民には知らされていましたが、山に隠れている日本兵は知りません。米軍のゴミ捨て場に食料を探しに山から降りて来て地雷を踏み、手足、首、胴体がバラバラになった日本兵の

死体が毎朝、何体も転がっていました。

阿佐の山の麓では、特攻隊員三十五人もの大量自決がありました。彼らは戦争中、阿佐村落の隠れ家に配置されていて、朝礼のときにはよく軍歌を歌っていました。特攻艇で米艦に体当たりすべく訓練されていた彼らは、一度も出撃することなく亡くなったのです。

朝鮮人軍夫（ぐんぷ）も空襲前までは五〜六人のグループで、監督に連れられて壕掘りに行く姿をよく見かけました。

夕方は自由解散になるのか、逃げ出してきたのか、大抵、一人でこっそりやって来て、垣根越しにこちらを覗（のぞ）き込んでいます。でも、入ってくることはしません。顔を洗わないのか真っ黒な汚れた顔をして、豚の餌（えさ）の芋を煮ていると、「少しでいいですからくれませんか？」と飯盒（はんごう）を差し出すので、よく芋を入れてあげた。

おなかがすいていたのでしょう。苦菜、蓬、野蒜など、食べられそうな野草を探しては口に入れていた姿が哀れでした。

慰安所「南風荘」の炊事係になって

兼島キクエ さん

かねしま・きくえ　一九二五年(大正十四年)九月生まれ。沖縄戦当時、父は南洋で漁師をしており、祖母、母、弟、双子の妹とともに阿嘉島で暮らしていた。「一〇・一〇空襲」を屋嘉比島で経験。その後、阿嘉島で慰安所の炊事係として働いた。米軍が上陸すると、手榴弾を使って家族で集団死しようとするが、祖母の一言をきっかけに思いとどまる。栄養失調で弱っていた弟は米軍の捕虜となった。兼島さんは難民として、一時慶留間島に強制移住となった。九十一歳。阿嘉島在住。

「死ぬときは一緒だよ!」と言った朝鮮の女の子たち

昭和十九年、私の父はカツオ船の漁師で、南洋のマーシャル諸島のヤルート島で仕事をしており、祖母、母と私、弟、双子の妹は阿嘉島で暮らしていました。

私は四人兄弟の長女だったので、小学校六年が終わると、阿嘉島や沖縄本島、屋嘉比島の銅山に子守りとして雇われました。また、慶留間島に草刈りの仕事にも出ました。

ある日、草刈りに行った慶留間島の母方の親類に、「阿嘉島では仕事もないだろう。パラオの水産会社で働かないか?」と言われました。

私が十四歳のときです。カツオ船の漁師さんたちと一緒に、私はパラオに行き働くことになりました。

当時、島では親が前渡し金をもらって、娘たちを「何年年季」といってパラオなどに年季奉公に出すという家もありましたが、私は親類の紹介ということもあって、年季奉公ではありませんでした。
パラオでは、水産会社の鰹節工場で働き、生魚から燻し、仕上げまでをやっていました。そのうちに戦況が厳しくなり、カツオ船が軍に徴用され工場も閉鎖されたので、しばらくは社長宅で女中奉公をしていました。
やがて、パラオの日本企業の引き揚げが始まり、昭和十九年四月の引き揚げ船に乗り、横浜港を経由して、私が阿嘉島に戻ったのは九月でした。

最初は、子守りで行ったことのある屋嘉比島の銅山の三号坑内で、四百人ほどの人たちと一緒に働きました。ダイナマイトで崩した鉱石をザルに入れ、坑内のトロッコで運ぶ仕事。坑内は狭くてザルを担げないので、トロッコまで引いて行くのがきつかった。

一番怖かったのは、「トロのピン抜き」でした。トロッコに鉱石を入れたら、急いでトロッコを止めているピンを抜いてやらないと、次のトロッコが来て止まっているトロッコに激突してしまいます。このピンを抜くタイミングが、とても難しかった。

「一〇・一〇空襲」は、屋嘉比島で経験。空襲は、パラオで二回経験しているので、低空飛行で向かってきたグラマン機の編隊を見て空襲を察知し、私は「逃げないと機銃掃射されるよ!」と叫びました。

すると、鉱山の現場監督に、「あれは米軍の演習だ。あんたが変なことを言うから、みんな坑内から出て行ったじゃないか」と怒られました。

ところが、突然、船に爆弾が落とされ、燃え上がったのを見て慌て出したのです。空襲で鉱山も仕事にならないと思い、夜、小舟を頼んで阿嘉島に戻りました。

島に戻ると、兵隊でいっぱい。村落の区長さんから、「慰安所の炊事婦をやってくれないか」と頼まれたので、引き受けました。
わが家のすぐ後方にある、立派な二軒の民家が慰安所として接収されており、そこには朝鮮人の女の子が七人いました。
まわりの民家もすべて軍が接収して、「基地中隊」「特幹部隊」「通信隊」など、隊ごとに入っていました。住民は、山の方に追い払われていました。
慰安所になった金城家と与那嶺家に、それぞれ三人と四人の女の子が一部屋ずつあてがわれ、その二軒を、兵隊たちは「南風荘」と呼んでいました。

炊事は、島の西側の人で子どももいる年配の人と二人でやりました。炊事係で大変だったのは、水汲みです。「南風荘」から一時間余りかけて、天秤棒の両端に一斗缶を下げて、二人で水を汲んで来るのです。
というのも、炊事だけでなく、彼女たちのために毎日、五右衛門風呂を

235 兼島キクエ

沸かさなければならなかったからです。彼女たちは体を洗ったり、お湯をかけたりしていましたが、ほとんど湯船に浸かるという習慣はありませんでした。

毎週金曜日は慰安所が休みで、「（性病の）検査の日」でした。昼から軍医が検診に来るので、風呂は午前中に沸かさなければなりません。風呂も炊事も、大きな与那嶺家でやっていました。

食糧は一週間分ずつ、軍の食糧庫に取りに行きます。米、味噌、油、コールタールのようなドロッとした黒糖の他は、おかず類はほとんどありません。

たまに、カレー用に冷凍のウサギ肉や蕗、蕨などの乾燥野草、缶詰などが入っていることもありました。でも、お酒だけは彼女たちのために配給されていました。

私は見たことはありませんが、私が帰った後、「午後から『兵隊』、夜は『上官』」などと時間を区切って、大勢が券を買って並んで順番を待っている」と、女の子たちが言っていました。一日に何人もの相手をする彼女たちは大変だったと思います。

身も心もくたくたになった彼女たちに「少しでも体を休めなさい」と言って、田舎の話や、親兄弟の話だけして帰る人もいたと。反対に、獣みたいな兵隊もいたと言っていました。

彼女たちは夜遅くまで働いているので朝は遅く、食事は昼と夜だけ。だから、夜食用のおにぎりを作って私たちは帰ります。食事が美味しくないときは、女の子たちが自分で「油味噌」を作って食べていました。味噌と黒糖を油で炒め、そこに朝鮮語で「タンレイ」という野蒜を刻んで入れていました。

彼女たちは比較的自由で、昼間は浜辺を散歩をしたり、ニシ浜にいく峠

237　兼島キクエ

を「アリラン峠」と呼んでそこに座り込み、海の方を見ていました。

若い女性七人なので結構、賑やかで、ふざけているのか本気なのか本当のことを言っていましたが、母国には帰れないと諦めていたようでした。

「キクエさん、死ぬときは一緒だよ!」などと威勢のいいことを言っていましたが、母国には帰れないと諦めていたようでした。

お酒が入ると、「キクエさんはこの島の人だからいいけど、私たちの故郷は遠いから……」と涙声になり、後はたいてい朝鮮語で愚痴を言い合ったりしていました。ケンカをすると、必ず朝鮮語になりました。

金城家には、ミハルさん（二十歳）とアケミさん、シノブさんの三人。

与那嶺家にはコユキさん、三十歳過ぎのコハナさん、やはり三十歳過ぎで、子どもを朝鮮に置いてきたというアキコさんがいました。

「軍需工場に働きに来たのが、こんな風になっちゃって」と、アキコさんは言っていました。もう一人、マチコさんは一番若く、十七歳か十八歳

だったと思います。来たばかりで日本語がまったく話せません。兵隊のことを「オッパ、オッパ（お兄さん、お兄さん）」と言っていました。あとの人は、二十四歳か二十五歳だったと思います。

三カ月ぐらいたった頃、全員、沖縄本島に行ってしまいました。軍のことなので、事前には何も知らされず、ある日、ご飯を作りに行ったら誰もいなかったのです。

その後、沖縄から戻った兵隊から彼女たちの消息を聞きました。多分、首里の司令部でミハルさんとコユキさんが死んでいたということです。親しかった上官が、気がかりで様子を見に行ったところを米軍に殺されたのでは、という話でした。

彼女たちで思い出すのは、軍が接収した阿嘉国民学校で「演芸会」があり、芸達者な兵隊が浴衣の尻をからげて安来節（ドジョウすくい）を踊った

り、黒田節を舞ったりしたのですが、そこで、「南風荘」の七人が「アリランの唄」を歌ったことです。兵隊たちは大喜びで、大好評でした。あとから、私もその歌を教えてもらいました。

阿嘉島には防空壕掘りの朝鮮人男性（軍夫）がたくさんいた。私たちは、「水勤隊（すいきんたい）」と呼んでいました。服装はバラバラで、軍服を着ている人もいれば、半ズボンに半袖シャツの朝鮮労働者の格好の人も。

一度、食料を盗んだという罪で、三人の水勤隊の人が後ろ手に縛（しば）られて山に連れて行かれるところを目撃しましたが、怖くて見ていられませんでした。後に、銃殺されたと聞きました。

米軍上陸後、「スパイだ」とか「食料を盗んだ」とか言って、日本軍が朝鮮労働者を酷（むご）い目に遭わせるのでかわいそうに思った染谷少尉や中島

中隊長が、生き残った水勤隊（軍夫）を連れて米軍本部に逃亡したという話を聞きました。

また、沖縄戦が終わると、阿嘉島の水勤隊も沖縄本島に帰ったのですが、コザの収容所では、自分たちをいじめた上官にみんなで復讐したという話も耳にしました。

三月二十三日からの大空襲の後、二十六日についに米軍が上陸。私たちは以前から、「米軍が上陸するとなぶり殺しにされるので、その前に自決する」ことになっていました。

阿嘉島は友軍の本部（司令部）があったので、兵隊と村落民は「ともに戦って、ともに死のう！」という、連帯意識のようなものがありました。弟も兵隊に、「死になさい！　早く自決しなさい！　自分がトドメを刺してあげますから。皆さんの死を見届けたら自分も米軍に切り込んで死にま

す！」と言ったそうです。
隣の慶留間島や渡嘉敷島のように、村落民だけに自決を強要するようなことはありませんでした。防衛隊の弟も、兵隊から自決用の手榴弾を五つぐらいもらって、持っていました。
「どうせ死ぬなら、皆で一カ所にまとまって死んだ方がいい」と、うちの家族と母の妹の家族を含めて十人ほどで中嶽のお宮の前で自決することになりました。
手榴弾は二個あったので、それぞれの家族が使うことにし、うちの家族は祖母、母と私、二人の妹の五人で輪になり、私が手榴弾のピンを抜こうとしました。
怖いという気持ちは全然、なかったです。一刻も早く死ねたらいい。しまないで死ねたらいい。そればかり考えていました。苦

ところが突然、祖母が、「防衛隊に行っている息子（母の弟）を一人残しては死ねない」と言って立ち上がり、フラフラと歩き出したのです。母がそのため結局、他の家族も「少し待ってみよう」と考え、自決を思いとどまったのでした。

ちょうどそこへ、防衛隊に行っていた母の弟（オバァの息子）がひょっこり戻って来ました。

そして、「村落の人たちはどこに行ったのかねぇ。全部、ここへ上がってきているのかい？」と島言葉で尋ねた。

オバァが、「他の村落の人たちは皆自決したんかね？」と聞くと、「生きてるよ。他の村落の人もまだ生きているよ」と答えたので、「じゃあ、死ぬのは少し待とう」ということになりました。

浜の方を見ると、ちょうど米軍の戦車が引き揚げていくところで、湾内

は米軍の軍艦やら船艇が、よくぶつからないものだ、と思うほどたくさん集まっていた。夜になってもこれらの船の明かりで、昼間のような明るさだったことを覚えています。

うちの家族は、山の中で友軍と三カ月ほど一緒にいました。桑の葉や芋の蔓（つる）など、食べられそうなものはすべて食べましたが、弟（十七歳）が栄養失調でだんだん弱ってきました。

わが家の唯一の跡取りである弟だけは、何としても死なすわけにはいきません。私は、捕虜になってでも弟を救おうと決めました。

でも、逃亡するところを日本兵に見つかると射殺されるので、夜の一時か二時頃、私は弟を連れて山を降りました。

着るものや身の回りの物など、持てるだけ持って山道を通って山の裏側のウタハ（大谷）に出て、私たちは米軍の捕虜になりました。

すぐに船艇に乗せられて、私は隣の慶留間島で降ろされましたが、弟は防衛隊員だったので、捕虜としてハワイまで連れて行かれました。

集団死で生き残った私

山川久子 さん

やまがわ・ひさこ　一九三八年(昭和十三年)五月生まれ。沖縄戦当時、祖父母と母、二人の弟と慶留間島に住んでいた。島民は、「米兵に捕まるとひどい目に遭わされる」と教えられており、米軍の上陸が始まると、家族は集団死するためにサーバルに向かう。大人がひもで子どもを死なせ、次に自分で自分の首を絞めて死ぬのだった。二人の弟が亡くなり、自身は息を吹き返した。この経験が重石となって胸の奥に残されたが、前を向いて精いっぱい生きた。七十八歳。那覇市在住。

「捕虜になってはいけない」と、暗に死を強要された

沖縄戦が始まったとき、父は防衛隊に召集されて家にはおらず、祖父母と母と私、四歳と二歳の弟で暮らしていました。
私たち家族が住んでいたのは、慶良間諸島の慶留間島の鎮守の森・大殿の近くです。
慶留間島は大きな阿嘉島と、小さな外地島の真ん中に位置する島で、当時、三つの島は橋がなく、繋がっていなかったのでサバニ（小舟）で行き来していました。
沖縄戦以前の慶留間島はカツオ漁が盛んで、「ケラマカツオ」という鰹節で有名だったのですが、戦争と共に廃れてしまいました。戦後、パラオやヤップ島から出稼ぎで戻ってきた人たちによって復活。父も鰹節を加工

する仕事をしていた。カツオの頭を落とし、四つに切り分けて、蒸し籠で炊いて、最後は松の木で燻して鰹節にするのです。加工場が港の近くにありました。

二月から四月にかけては、ザトウクジラの群れが奥武島の辺りを泳いでいくのが見えました。クジラの頭が黒いコブのように並んで海を進んでいくのです。

慶留間島には、五月の「豊作祈願の祭り」と八月の海の「大漁祈願の祭り」がありました。

百人余りの島民は皆、血が繋がっていて、家系をたどるとほとんどが親類になるということです。

「豊作祈願の祭り」には米を石臼で挽いて粉にし、それを蒸かしてどぶろくを作り、村の大殿鎮にお供えしてから、みんなで豊作を願って飲みます。

「大漁祈願の祭り」は「イビ」という屋形に集まって女たちがオモロ（想

い）歌を歌い、輪太鼓を打って踊った後、浜で男たちが輪になって大漁を願って酒盛りをするのです。

慶留間島の人は、隣の阿嘉島に田んぼを持っていることが多く、田植えや稲刈りの時期にはサバニを漕いで行くのです。大人たちが田んぼで作業をしている間、私はカエルを取ったりトンボを追いかけたりしていました。島の周囲は一時間もあれば回ることができたでしょうが、道は阿嘉島へ抜ける一本道しかないので、回ってみたことはありません。

阿嘉島側のアカムティというところに、陸軍特攻艇（マルレ＝連絡艇の意）の基地があり、そこは秘密の場所になっていて、島民は近寄ってはいけないことになっていました。朝鮮人労働者や慰安婦などもいたと後に聞きましたが、私は見たことはありません。

軍の司令部は阿嘉島にあるので、何かあると上官と副官の二人が来て、

村の分教場に住民を集め、「米軍が上陸して来ても、絶対に捕虜になってはいけない」と、暗に自決を強要。それ以前にも兵隊が何度か来て、「米軍が上陸すると男はひどい目に遭わされ、女は辱（はずかし）めを受ける」などと〝洗脳教育〟をしていたといいます。

「一〇・一〇空襲」のその日、父のいとこが出征することになり、わが家で壮行会が開かれました。天ぷらを揚げたり芋餅をついたりと、皆で準備をしているとき、飛行機が四機、編隊を組んで飛んできた。友軍の飛行機だと思って、皆が外に出て手を振りました。

ところが、父のいとこが「あれは敵機だ！」と言ったのでビックリ。それが、戦争の幕開けだったのです。

やがて、『一〇・一〇空襲』で那覇が焼け野原になった」との知らせが入ったので、島でも避難壕（ごう）を造ることになりました。

最初はタコツボのような縦穴を掘り、入り口に階段をつけて、中に降りてゆく形です。天井に細板を組み、その上に萱を葺いた蓋を作りましたが、米軍が上陸したら役に立たないということが分かり、水のあるウンジャ河原の山に横穴を掘り、やはり萱でカモフラージュした扉を立てかけました。ここは椎の木の林だったので、椎の実がたくさん落ちており、私たちは椎の実を食事代わりに食べていました。

慶留間島への最初の爆撃は、三月二十三日。この日は、学校と民家四軒が爆撃で焼かれました。この五軒には電話線が通っていて、敵機は島の通信を止めるために破壊したのです。

年寄りと女、子ども、それに区長しかいないような島でしたが、十四～十六歳までの五人の中学生がいました。彼らは、島の「伝令」として山の

上で見張りに立ち、米軍の上陸を発見するとアカムティの基地に知らせに行き、また、基地の命令をウンジャ河原の住民に知らせる、という役割で島内を駆け回っていました。

二十三日に続き、翌二十四、二十五日は朝から海上と空からの爆撃が続きました。そして、三月二十六日未明まで続き、朝の八時頃でピタリと攻撃はやんだのです。上空の爆撃機も爆弾を落とさなくなりました。米軍の上陸が始まっていたのでした。

ウンジャ河原の避難壕にいた私たちのところに、「伝令」が「サーバルではすでに自決を始めています」と知らせに来ました。

私たち家族はウンジャ河原の祖母方の避難壕にいたので、そこを出て皆と一緒に自決場所を探しにゾロゾロと歩き出した。すると、「あんた方は祖父方の人たちと行くべきだ」と言われたので、父方の親類を追ってサー

バルの方へ向かいました。

祖母方の家族たちは島の断崖のあるアタクバラに向かい、ほとんどの人が木で首を括(くく)って自決。二人の子どもを殺して死のうとした両親が死にきれず、米軍に保護されたときは、二人とも正気を失っていたということでした。

死のうと思っても死ねなかった人たちがほかにも、海岸を彷徨(さまよ)っているところを米軍に保護されたりしたそうです。

サーバルには上下二つの壕があって、自決は主に上の壕で行われました。壕に着くと、軍艦が大好きな上の弟は、「友軍の軍艦を見る!」と言って、トコトコと丘の方へ行き、海の米艦を眺めはじめたのです。祖父がそっと後ろから近づき、すくい上げるように弟を抱き上げ、壕の中に入りました。壕の中では、すでに多くの人が紐(ひも)で首を絞められて、一斉に足を入り口

に向けて死んでいました。殺した孫をおぶったまま、正座して死んでいる老婆や、苦しかったのか壁をかきむしり、寄りかかって死んでいる人もいました。皆、絞殺でした。

渡嘉敷島は刃物で自決した人が多く、凄惨を極めました。友軍から手榴弾をもらったところは手榴弾で自決したため、手足が吹き飛んだり腹が裂けたりしてむごたらしかったと言います。

慶留間島では手榴弾をもらった人は一人もいませんでした。同じ自決でも、慶留間島は血を流さなかっただけ、まだ良かった、と言うしかありません。

島民がなぜ、絞殺を選んだのかというと、「一〇・一〇空襲」の少し前に、島に仕事で来た人が寝床の中で、紐で自分の首を絞めて自殺しているのを発見されたことがありました。それが記憶にあって、「死ぬのなら絞

殺がいい」と皆が思い込んでいたようです。
実際は、男たちが女、子どもを先に殺し、次に自分の首を絞めるのですが、これがなかなか難しいのです。顔色はチアノーゼ反応で紫色になり、顔面が丸く腫れ上がるけれど、そこから絶命とまでは、なかなかいかないのです。ですから、サーバルでも父親や息子が残り、母親と娘が殺された家がいくつもありました。

私は絞殺されることは知っていました。祖父が、すでに死んでいる親類の叔母さんの首に巻いてあった紐を外して、「私たちもすぐに後から行くからね」と言ったのを聞いたからです。
祖母は無表情で自分の帯を解き、三本に裂いて紐を作っていました。母はモンペなので帯を締めていないし、祖父の作業着の帯は硬くて裂けなかったからです。

258

祖父は、私のオカッパ頭を撫でながら首に紐を巻きつけ、一気に絞めました。私はとっさに、「死にたくない。お父ぅメーカイ（父さんのところに）イチュンドウ（行く）」と言って首をさかんに振ったので、結び目に少し隙間ができたようです。締められた瞬間、一瞬、気絶しましたがすぐに気が付き、ぼんやりと周囲は見えていました。

祖父がその後、上の弟を。母は下の弟にオッパイを飲ませながら絞殺しました。その後、祖父、祖母、母は自分たちで紐を使って首を絞めましたが、なかなか死にきれないのです。

そのとき、「出テキナサイ」「出テキナサイ」と、呼びかける日系二世の声と一緒に、親類の中学生の「伝令」が壕の入り口に姿を現した。

私は入り口に足を向けて倒れていたので、すぐに分かりました。「ヨネヒロ兄さんが呼んでるよ」と、息を吹き返した私が叫んだので、祖父も祖母も自決を中止。

259　山川久子

母はすでに失神していたので、ヨネヒロ兄さんと一緒に来た人が母の頬を何度も平手打ちして蘇生させました。

私は祖父を恨んではいません。むしろ大好きな祖父でした。祖父との思い出はたくさんあります。私は初孫だったので、とてもかわいがってくれ、阿嘉島の田んぼに行くときはいつも、船尾で船を漕ぐ祖父の前に私を座らせます。お正月の三が日は、ヤギの餌になる草刈りに外地島に行くのが恒例で、帰りの船いっぱいに積んだ青草の匂いが祖父との思い出と重なります。

外地島の開墾は、萱を刈って燃やし、そこにスイカや冬瓜の苗を植えるのですが、苗が枯れないように、祖父は一つ一つ手を取って、丁寧に植え方を教えてくれたものです。

島で生き残った五十余人の人たちは、誰が誰を殺したのかを知っていました。ですから、終戦直後は、重苦しくやり切れない空気が島中に漂っていました。

でも、いつまでも過去にとらわれているわけにはいきません。忘れたわけではありませんが、自分たちが生きていくので精いっぱいでした。

母はその後、しばらく男の子ができなかったのです。

あるとき、祖母が何気なく「男の子ができないのは、長男、次男を殺めた罰かね」と、つぶやきました。それを聞いた母は、大声で泣きました。私は胸にいつも重石を抱えていました。母が亡くなったので、もう、語ってもいいかもしれないと思い、お話しいたしました。

むすびにかえて

創価学会沖縄青年部は、沖縄戦七十年となった二〇一五年から、戦争の記憶の継承、そして、平和を愛する「沖縄の心」を継承することを目的に「ONEからはじまる」をテーマに掲げ平和運動を展開してきました。

この「ONE」には、「一人から」、「ワンから」（沖縄のことばで自分のこと）、そして、世界中の友と平和を求める心を「一つ」にしていくことで、世界の平和を実現できるとの思いが込められています。

二〇一五年三月には、宜野湾市の沖縄コンベンションセンターに八千人が集い「世界青年平和大会 OKINAWA ピースウェーブフェスタ2

015」を開催しました。この大会の席上、沖縄青年部が大会を目指し取り組んできた三万を超す平和意識調査の発表を行い、戦争体験を学び・残し・伝えていく」運動を決意し合いました。そして、「沖縄戦の体験を学び・残し・伝えていく」運動を開始しました。

また、六月には、創価学会沖縄研修道場にある「世界平和の碑」の前で青年平和主張大会を開催、東京・広島・長崎から集った青年とともに、世界平和の実現へ「命こそ宝」の精神を世界に発信しました。

今回、発刊する運びとなった『未来へつなぐ平和のウムイ（思い）――沖縄戦を生き抜いた14人の真実』は、この二つの大会に参加した青年が中心となって開催した「ピースフォーラム（戦争体験を聞く会）」などで、沖縄戦の生存者から伺った証言を収めたものです。

中米・コスタリカ共和国の元大統領でノーベル平和賞受賞者のオスカル・アリアス・サンチェス博士は、かつて、「他人の苦境に同苦し、きた

263

るべき世代の幸福を思いやれる、道徳的な勇気と、障害がいかに大きくとも、必ず現実は変革できるとの希望と確信」を世界市民の条件としてあげられました。

 島の地形が変わるほど砲弾を浴びせられ、約二十万人が犠牲となり、米軍の戦史に「ありったけの地獄を集めた」と刻まれた沖縄戦を学ぶことによって、今もなお、世界各地で紛争の犠牲になっている人たちの苦しみに同苦することができます。

 そして、何よりも平和こそ私たちの幸福の第一歩であることを、次の世代に受け継ぐことができます。さらに、現在では、世界中から観光客が訪れるまでに発展した沖縄の姿そのものが、戦争ですべてを破壊され絶望の底にいる人たちへ、再建への夢と確信を与えることができると信じます。

 池田SGI（創価学会インタナショナル）会長は、「戦火のやまぬ世界に、最も必要な太陽こそ『沖縄の心』」と言われました。私たち沖縄青年部は、

世界市民の自覚で、世界の友と手をとりあい、世界平和の実現のために「沖縄の心」を世界に広げてまいります。

最後に、本書の出版に尽力された沖縄青年平和委員会、女性平和文化会議、第三文明社の皆様に心から感謝申し上げます。

　二〇一六年九月

　　　　　　　　　創価学会沖縄青年部長　中村武夫

future generations, and to work with inspiration and determination to change our situation, no matter how difficult it may be."

During the Battle of Okinawa, the islands were hit so hard by bombs and artillery they actually changed shape. More than 200,000 people were killed in situations that manifested "all the possible hells" of US military history. Learning about the Battle of Okinawa allows us to share the suffering of those who, today, face similar horrible circumstances in war and armed conflict around the world. Above all, we learned that peace is the first, prerequisite step for our own happiness and that of coming generations. Okinawa has recovered to become a beautiful, prosperous location attracting tourists from all over the world. Okinawa can help people understand the deep despair that comes with the total destruction of war while maintaining hope and determination for recovery.

SGI President Daisaku Ikeda once said, "What we most need in this world of ceaseless war is the spirit of Okinawa." The Okinawa Youth Division will, as citizens of the world working hand in hand with friends everywhere, spread the spirit of Okinawa to promote genuine world peace.

In closing we express our deepest gratitude to the Okinawa Youth Peace Committee, the Young Women's Conference for Peace and Culture and DAISANBUNMEI-SHA, Inc. for their contributions to the publication of this book.

September 2016
Takeo Nakamura
Director
Soka Gakkai Okinawa Youth Division

In Closing

In 2015, the 70th anniversary of the Battle of Okinawa, the Okinawa Youth Division launched a peace campaign with the theme "Peace Starts from ONE." The goal is to pass on memories of the war and the peace-loving "spirit of Okinawa." ONE in the Okinawan dialect means "myself," so this slogan expresses our hope that the desire for peace in each ONE of us will join with others and bring genuine peace to the world.

We held an "International Youth Festival for Peace– Peace Wave Festa 2015" in the Okinawa Convention Center, Ginowan City in March that drew 8,000 youth. At this conference, the Okinawa Youth Division presented the results of a peace attitude survey of over 30,000 individuals. All attendees affirmed their determination to pass on the war experience, and we launched a new campaign to "learn, leave and communicate the Battle of Okinawa."

In June, we held a Peace Festa in front of the Monument to World Peace in the Soka Gakkai Okinawa Dojo. We affirmed our plans to work for world peace and sent out Okinawa's cry against war. Young people from Tokyo, Hiroshima, Nagasaki and around Japan agreed: "Life is a treasure."

Thinking Peace is a collection of testimonies we heard from survivors of the Battle of Okinawa during a peace forum featuring war experiences communicated to the young people who attended the two meetings mentioned above. Dr. Oscar Arias Sanchez, former President of Republic of Costa Rica and Nobel Peace Prize laureate, once suggested that world citizenship is "the spirit of virtuous courage that allows us to share the hardships of others, envision happiness for

my hand and carefully taught me how to plant and keep them from withering.

The fifty or so people who survived on our island always knew who killed who. Therefore, when the war ended, the island was filled with an unbearable, oppressive tension. But we can't live in the past forever. I have forgotten nothing, but it was all I could do just to survive.

My mother had no baby boy for long time after that. One time my grandma muttered, "We can't have a boy. This is our punishment for killing the boys we had." Hearing that, my mother cried out loud.

I have carried this heavy stone in my mind. But my mother passed away in May 2014. That's when I thought maybe it's time to speak and release my stone.

too hard to tear off.

Smoothing my bobbed hair, grandfather wound a string around my neck and throttled me in one stroke. Just before that I quickly said, "I don't want to die. I'll go to my father's place," and as he pulled, I shook my neck hard. It seems the knot must have loosened a bit. I lost consciousness for a moment, but soon I came to and was able to see in the dim light what was going on around me.

Grandfather killed my younger brother. My mother nursed my youngest brother, then strangled him herself. After that, grandfather, grandmother and mother attempted to strangle themselves using the three strings. But they were having a terrible time getting it done.

Just then, I heard the voice of a Japanese-American calling, "Come out," in Japanese. At the same time, a junior high relative who had been a messenger showed up at the entrance of the cave. Because I was laid down with my legs toward the entrance, I saw him right away. I came to and shouted, "Yonehiro is calling us." My grandparents stopped trying to kill themselves. My mother was already unconscious, but Yonehiro and his companion slapped her cheek several times and revived her.

I have no resentment against my grandfather. I have always loved him. I have numerous fond memories of him. I was his first grandchild, and he took special care of me. Every time when he went to the rice fields on Aka Island, he sat in the stern, rowing our Sabani, and he let me sit right in front of him. During the first three days of the new year, we always went to Fukaji Island to cut grass to feed our goats. The smell of green grass filling the boat on the way home is connected in my memory with my grandfather.

When we worked the land on Fukaji Island, we mowed and burnt thatch, planting watermelon and white squash. My grandfather took from behind and lifted him by his arms as if to let him swing. He brought him back to the cave.

Inside the cave, many people had already been strangled with string. The dead were laid out with their legs toward the entrance. One old lady was dead but still sitting on her knees carrying the grandchild she had just killed on her back. May be it was so hard, a person scratched the wall and died leaning on it. All of them were killed by strangulation.

On Tokashiki Island, most people killed themselves with knives. I heard it was extremely bloody and gruesome. Some were given grenades by the Japanese Army. Their arms and legs were blown away and their organs came out. That, too, was horrible.

On Geruma Island, nobody got a grenade. We did commit suicide. There's no other word for it, but at least we didn't spill our blood on our island. We chose strangulation because just before the October 10 air raid, someone had come to work on our island but was found in bed having killed himself with a string. Many of us remembered that and thought, "If I have to die, that would be a good way."

To tell the truth, what happened is, the men killed the women and children first, then they strangled themselves, but strangling yourself is extremely difficult. Their faces swelled up round and turned purple, but they passed out and let go before they actually died. Therefore, in many cases, mothers and daughters died but fathers and sons survived.

I knew I would be strangled. My grandfather took a string from around my aunt's neck. I heard him tell her, "We'll follow you soon." Grandmother's face was like stone. She untied her sash and tore it into three strings. She had to make three strings because my mother wore *monpe* work pants, which had no sash, and my grandfather's sash was

On our island were mostly women, children, some elderly men and a village chief. We did have five junior high students 14 to 16. They ran around the island serving as messengers. They also stood watch on the mountain. When they saw the US coming, they went to the base in Akamuty to tell the Army. Then, they took orders from the base to the people who had taken shelter in the cave on the Unja River.

After the bombing on March 23, more bombing and artillery fire from the ocean continued through the 24 and 25. The attack lasted until just before dawn on the 26. At around 8:00 that morning, it suddenly stopped completely. US bombers stopped dropping bombs. The US invasion began.

A messenger came to our cave at Unja River and said, "In Sabaru they've started the suicide." My family and I had taken refuge in a cave with relatives on my mother's side. When we heard the message, we all left the cave and began looking as a group for a place to commit mass suicide. Then someone said, "You should be with your father's side." So we headed toward Sabaru, following our father's relatives.

My mother's relatives headed toward Atakubara cliff. Most of them hung themselves in trees. Two parents intended to kill themselves after they killed their two children, but they failed. When they were taken custoday by the US Army, they were both quite insane. I heard about others who failed in their suicide attempts wandering the beaches until they were taken custoday by the US.

Sabaru had upper and lower caves; the suicides took place mainly in the upper cave. When we arrived, my brother, who loved warships, said, "I'll go and see our Army's warships!" He trotted up the hill to watch US warships in the ocean. Grandfather approached him gently

residents to assemble in the village school. One time they told us, "If the US invades this island, you must never allow yourselves to be taken prisoner." They were strongly implying that we should commit suicide. I heard that even before that time, soldiers had come several times to brainwash us. "When the US invades the island, men will be tortured and women will be raped." This was their message.

On October 10, the day of the big air raid, my father's cousin was called up for military service and came to our house to say goodbye. We had a farewell party for him. We were preparing tempura, pounding potato cakes and cooking other food when four airplanes flew over in formation. We thought they were Japanese planes, so we all went out and waved.

My father's cousin said, "No, those are enemy planes." We were shocked. That was the beginning of the war for us. Soon we learned that Naha was burned to the ground by the October 10 air raid. We decided to build a trench to hide in.

We dug a pit, like an octopus trap. We built stairs at the entrance so we could climb down into it. We made a ceiling of wooden boards and a door covered with thatch. However, we soon learned that our shelter would be useless if the US actually invaded our island. Instead, we dug a large cave in the mountain near the Unja River. We covered the door with leaves so it looked just like the mountain side. This cave was in a chinquapin forest, so we had plenty of chinquapin nuts lying around on the ground. We ate mostly chinquapin nuts after that.

The first air raid on Geruma Island was on March 23. A school building and four houses were destroyed. These five buildings had telephone lines so the US destroyed them to cut communication to and from our island.

pieces, heat it in a steam basket, then smoke it with pine wood. Some processing plants were near the port.

From February to April, we could see schools of humpback whales swimming around Oh Island. Their heads appeared like groups of large black bumps moving over the ocean.

Geruma's population was a little over a hundred, and we were all related. We can trace our family line to show that nearly all of us have some sort of blood connection.

On Geruma Island, we have a Harvest Festival in May and a Large Catch Festival in August. For the Harvest Festival, we grind rice to powder in a stone hand mill. The powder is steamed and used to make home-brewed *sake*. After offering the sake to our village shrine and praying for good crop, the villagers drink the *sake*.

For the Big Catch Festival, the women get together in a sacred spot, sing a song that expresses their desire for fishing success, beat drums and dance. The men sit in a circle on the beach where they pray for a big catch, then enjoy a drinking party.

Many people on Geruma Island had rice fields on Aka Island, so they rowed their Sabani there for planting and harvest. While the adults were working in the rice fields, I caught frogs or chased dragonflies. I believe I could walk around Aka Island in an hour, but there was only one road, and that cut across the island, so I never have walked around the whole island.

An Army Kamikaze base was located in an area called Akamuty on the Aka Island side of Geruma. That base was top secret and islanders were forbidden to approach it. I later heard that Korean laborers and comfort women were there, but I never saw them.

Army headquarters were on Aka Island, so when they had something to tell us, a senior officer and an adjutant would call the

I survived mass suicide

Hisako Yamagawa
Born May 1938. At the time of the Battle of Okinawa, living on Geruma Island with grandparents, mother and two younger brothers. The Japanese Army told islanders they would be tortured if captured by Americans. When the US invasion started, Hisako and her family headed for Sabaru to take part in a mass suicide. Adults killed children, then killed themselves. Her two brothers were killed, but she survived. This experience has been a heavy stone in her mind, but she did her best to live positively. Seventy-eight, living in Naha City.

We were told, "Don't let them take you prisoner," which meant, "Commit suicide"

When the Battle of Okinawa started, my father was already drafted into the Defense Corps, so he was away from home. I lived with my grandparents, my mother, and my younger brothers, who were four and two.

We lived near a village shrine called Ufudonchi on Geruma Island in the Kerama Island Chain. Geruma is between Aka Island to the north and Fukaji Island to the south. The three islands were not connected by bridges at that time, so we went back and forth in small boats called Sabani.

Before the Battle of Okinawa, Geruma was a great place to catch bonito. We were famous for a form of dried bonito called Kerama Bonito. The bonito catch declined as the war dragged on. After the war, people who had gone to work in Palau or Yap came back and revived the industry. My father was also involved in processing bonito. To make dried bonito, you cut off the head, cut the flesh into four

effects as possible, we walked down a mountain road to Utaha. There, we were taken prisoner by the US Army.

We were immediately taken to a boat. They put me off at Geruma Island. My brother, who was in the Defense Corps, was sent to Hawaii.

pin from the grenade. I had no feeling of fear. I hope I can die instantly. I hope I can die without suffering. That was all I was thinking.

Suddenly, Grandma said, "I can't go and leave my son (mother's younger brother)." She stood up and started to stagger away. My mother followed her. I was compelled to follow them. Because of my grandmother, the whole family thought, "We better wait." In the end, we abandoned the idea of committing suicide.

Just then, my mother's younger brother (Grandma's son) in Defense Corps, came back. He asked, "Where is everybody? Is the community up here?"

Grandma asked, "Have the people in other communities committed suicide?"

He answered, "They're alive. Most of the people in other communities are still alive."

So we said, "Then let's wait."

As I looked toward the beach, US tanks were pulling up. A huge number of US warships and boats were in the bay, so many I wondered, "How can they keep from crashing into each other?" I remember that night was as bright as day because of the light from those ships.

My family stayed with Japanese troops in the mountains for about three months. We ate everything and anything, including mulberry leaves and potato runners. My younger brother, who was 17, was getting weaker and weaker for lack of food. My brother was the only male heir in my family. I could not possibly let him die. I decided to save him, even if it meant being taken prisoner.

However, I knew we would be killed by Japanese soldiers if they saw us running away. I decided to take my brother down the mountain at one or two in the morning. Taking as many clothes and personal shot.

After the US invasion of Okinawa, I heard that the Japanese Army tortured Korean laborers, claiming they were spies or stole food, Second Lieutenant Sometani and Company Commander Nakajima, who sympathized them, took surviving SWSC laborers and sought refuge at US Army Headquarters.

I also heard that after the Battle of Okinawa was over, the SWSC assigned to Aka Island went back to Okinawa. They were taken to the POW camp in Koza (now, Okinawa City) with Japanese soldiers. Some got together to take revenge on senior officers who had treated them badly.

The great air raid on our island started on March 23. The US landed on the 26. We had decided to commit suicide before the US could capture and torture us. We had a Japanese Army headquarters on our island, and our community and the soldiers shared a sense of solidarity "We're ready to fight and die together!" My younger brother told a soldier, "Kill yourself. Hurry up! I'll finish you off. I'll fight my way into the US troops and die after I know everyone else is dead!"

There was no compulsion or any demand for suicide by residents, as there was on Geruma and Tokashiki islands. A soldier gave my brother, who served in the Defense Corps, five grenades to be used for suicide.

About ten of us, including my family and my mother's younger sister's family, decided to commit suicide in front of the shrine on Mt. Naka. We said, "If we're going to kill ourselves, it's better to do it together."

We had two grenades so each family could use one. My grandma, mother, two sisters, and I sat in a circle, and I was just about to pull the

Kohana and Akiko were over thirty. Akiko had left a child in Korea. They and Koyuki were assigned to Yonamine.

Akiko used to say, "I came to work for a munitions factory but I ended up doing this." Machiko was the youngest. I think she was seventeen or eighteen. She had just come to Japan and couldn't speak Japanese at all. She called soldiers "oppa," meaning "young man." Akemi, Shinobu, and Koyuki were around twenty-four or five.

After about three months passed, all of them were gone to Island of Okinawa. This was a military deployment so we knew nothing in advance. One day I went to prepare a meal, and nobody was there. I heard what happened later from a soldier who had come back from Okinawa. Miharu and Koyuki were killed when the headquarters in Shuri was bombed. He said they had probably gone to see a senior officer they had known well and were killed by a US attack.

I remember an art festival in Aka Elementary School, which was controlled by the Army. A versatile entertainer-soldier tucked up the hem of his kimono into his sash and performed a humorous loach-scooping dance. The seven women from South Wind Lodge sang Arirang. The soldiers enjoyed it very much. It was a big hit. I learned that song from them later.

Many male Korean laborers had to dig shelters on Aka Island. Their unit was the Special Water Service Company, which we called the SWSC. Their dress was not unified. Some wore military uniforms. Others wore Korean laborer-style short-sleeved undershirts and shorts.

I once ran across three SWSC laborers tied with their hands behind their backs charged with stealing food. They were being taken to the mountain. I couldn't bear to look at them. Later I heard they were canned food. Alcoholic drinks were given to the comfort women.

I never saw the actual rooms, but the girls told me, "Our time is divided –soldiers in the afternoon, senior officers at night. Lots of them buy tickets and wait their turn in line." After I went home each night, I am sure they had a hard time dealing with such a large number of soldiers.

The girls were exhausted, physically and mentally. Some soldiers said, "You need to rest," and they just talked to them for a while about their hometowns and families. Others were like animals.

They worked until late at night so their morning started late. They ate only lunch and supper. We made rice balls for midnight snacks, then left home. When they found a meal we made not tasty enough, they cooked for themselves, usually "lard and miso saute," which they ate with rice. "Lard and miso saute" is an Okinawan dish made by stir-frying miso and brown sugar with lard. As their specialty, they added Korean rocambole, if they had it.

They were relatively free. They strolled on the beach. They named a mountain ridge on the way to Nishi Beach "Arirang Pass." They sat there watching the ocean during their free time. Because seven young women were living together, they were quite lively. I didn't know if they were joking or not when they said, "We'll all be together when we die, Kikue!" It sounded bold, but I knew it meant they had given up on going back to their homeland.

When they drank alcohol, they used to say, "It's OK for you, Kikue. You're from here. Our homes are far away…" By the time they finished saying things like this, they were crying. Later on, they complained about their circumstances in Korean. Whenever they argued, it was always in Korean.

Miharu was twenty. She, Akemi and Shinobu were assigned to Kinjo.

job, I hired a small boat and returned to Aka Island that night.

Soldiers were everywhere on our island. The community chief asked me if I would work as a cook in the comfort station. I accepted. Two magnificent private residences just behind my house had been seized for comfort stations. They had seven Korean girls.

Other private houses around my house were all seized by the military, each occupied by "Base Company" or "Special Staff" or "Communications Unit." The residents were driven away to the mountains.

Three or four girls were allocated one room each at the Kinjo and Yonamine residences, converted to comfort stations. Soldiers called these two houses South Wind Lodge.

I cooked with an older woman who had children and lived in the western part of the island. My most difficult task as a cook was carrying water. Two of us carried water in two big buckets hanging on both ends of a shoulder pole. Each trip took over an hour.

Two of us had to do this because, in addition to the water we needed for cooking, we had to fill and warm the bath every day. They used hot water to wash their bodies, but I think the Koreans weren't used to soaking in the bath.

Every Friday was off at the comfort station. That was the day for venereal disease testing. An army doctor would come to do the examinations in the afternoon so we had to fill the bath in the morning. We used the kitchen and the bath in the large Yonamine residence.

We went to get food from the Army depot every week. We got rice, miso paste, oil and sticky coal-tar-like brown sugar. We rarely got anything for extra side dishes. Occasionally, we got frozen rabbit for curry, a dried wild herb like butterbur or bracken or sometimes some apprenticeships. But my work came through a relative. I was not going for an apprenticeship.

I worked for a bonito processing factory run by a marine products company. I started with living fish and went right through drying to finishing. In the meantime, the war was getting worse. Bonito boats were being commandeered by the military, and our factory shut down. After that, I worked for a while as a maid at the president's house.

Eventually, Japanese companies operating in Palau started returning to Japan. I boarded a "repatriation ship" that left Palau in April 1944. I returned by way of Yokohama; it was September before I got back to Aka Island.

There, I worked in pit number 3 of the copper mine on Yakabi Island where I had gone for babysitting. About four hundred workers were there. My job was to put the ore blasted to bits by dynamite into a huge colander and carry it to a railcar in the pit. The pit was very narrow. I couldn't carry the colander on my shoulder, so it was extremely hard to pull it to the railcar.

The scariest task was "unpinning" the railcar. After we filled a car with ore, we had to quickly remove the pin holding the car we had filled or the next car would arrive and crash into it. The timing for that unpinning was quite difficult.

I experienced the October 10 air raid on Yakabi Island. I had experienced two air raids in Palau. Seeing the Grumman airplanes flying in low, I knew it was a raid, so I shouted, "Run! Their guns will get us!"

The site manager scolded me. "This is just a drill. You made everyone run out of the pit because with your ridiculous warning."

Just then, a bomb fell on a boat and it burst into flame. Now my manager was even more upset. Thinking the raid would cost me my

Cooking for a comfort station

Kikue Kaneshima
Born September 1925. At the time of the Battle of Okinawa, her father was fishing in the Marshall Islands. She lived with her grandmother, mother, younger brother and twin sisters on Aka Island. Experienced the October 10 air raid on Yakabi Island. Worked as a cook at the comfort station on Aka Island. After the US invasion, her family was about to commit suicide using a grenade, but her grandmother changed their minds. To rescue her brother, who was weakened by malnutrition, they became prisoners. Ninety-one years old, living on Aka Island.

The Korean women said, "We'll all be together when we die!"

In 1944, my father was on a bonito boat working the Jaluit Atoll in the Marshall Islands. I lived with my grandmother, mother, younger brother, and twin sisters on Aka Island. I was twenty years old.

Because I was the first of four siblings, when I completed sixth grade in elementary school I went to work taking care of children for workers at the copper mines on islands of Aka, Yakabi and Okinawa. I also helped with the cutting of grass and weeds on Geruma Island.

One day, I was helping a relative on my mother's side cutting weeds on Geruma Island when he asked, "You can't get much work on Aka, can you? Would you like to work for a marine products company in Palau?"

That was in 1938, when I was 14. So I went to Palau with some bonito fishermen who were going to Palau to bring their families back to Okinawa. In those days, some families on our island received payments in advance to send their daughters to Palau for from Asa were allowed to go back to their community. Ama people remained in their community.

Around that time, the US Army became angry at the Japanese soldiers hiding in the mountains. They buried land mines on N'chara Beach. A refuse dump was created at the US camp in Kozamami. They threw pots and pans, edible ham and sausage, and other useful items into the dump. We were in desperate need on the island, so residents were allowed to take things from the dump. Japanese soldiers in mountains also found out about the food in the US dump.

Island residents were informed about the land mines on the beach, but hold-out Japanese soldiers were not. Several bodies with arms, legs, and heads broken into pieces were found every morning. They came down from the mountains to the US dump to look for food and stepped on the land mines.

In Asa, 35 soldiers of kamikaze troops committed suicide. They had been living in houses in Asa. During morning assemblies they sang military songs. They were trained to drive their kamikaze boats right into US warships, but this group killed themselves without ever going on a mission.

I saw some Korean laborers several times. Before the air raid, I saw five or six of them led by a Japanese supervisor going down to dig a cave. There was one who came around in the evening. I wondered if he was freed or escaped. He looked quietly over the hedge into my yard. He didn't come in. I wondered why he didn't wash his face, it was so dirty. Several times when I was cooking potatoes for big dinner, he held out his mess tin and said, "Would you give me just a little bit?" I put some potatoes in his mess tin. I think he was hungry. I saw him picking edible weeds.

At the entrance to Yuhina Cave, the Women's Association was growing radishes and carrots. We picked some and ate them raw.

A young woman went into labor in the cave. Her family was caring for her anxiously. A few days later, she started actually giving birth. My grandma and mother took her into the Adan palm grove and helped her deliver the baby. I consider that delivery a great achievement.

Around that time, the US Army frequently dropped leaflets from airplanes saying, "The war is over. It is safe to come out."

Mr. Uehara, the head of our community, said, "We can surrender now and we won't be killed. Let's go. Don't worry." A Japanese soldier heard him say that. When Mr. Uehara went home to get something, a soldier was waiting for him. The soldier shot and killed him.

My family and I, together with my uncle's family, more than ten of us altogether, found a big cave between the Nunruru and Yuhina caves. We moved in there. We climbed Mt. Akazaki to watch what was happening during the day, returning to sleep in the cave at night. Rotting bodies of Japanese soldiers killed by bombs and artillery were strewn all over the mountain.

By that time, the island was firmly under US control. American soldiers appeared to be having fun on launches in the bay of Ago, but they were actually watching the island.

One day, a soldier on a launch saw my mother. She hurried back to cave, but the soldier informed headquarters, and jeeps came to our cave. We were all taken prisoner.

The men were taken to Army headquarters in Zamami Village, where they were thoroughly investigated to see if they were civilians or soldiers. Anyone found to be a soldier was sent to Hawaii. Women and children had to get off the jeep in Ama. Several days later, people

In a goat pen near my house, I saw more than ten soldiers and young men from the island killed by a bomb. After the US invasion started on March 26, the Japanese soldiers remaining on the island fled into the mountains. No soldiers were seen in the village.

My mother and sister came to Nunruru Cave, where I was, but we had no food. My mother and a few other people went to steal rice from the Japanese Army. It was stored in a nearby cave. This cave was actually in the ocean when the tide was high, so they could only go in when the tide was low. The cave was a storm shelter for tuna boats.

According to my mother, a lot of soldiers killed themselves in the storage cave. Their bodies filled the entrance. It was dark inside. She felt around for a straw bag of rice and found a whole pile of them. Fifteen or sixteen bodies lay on top of the bags. When she pushed them with her foot to get them off the rice, the bodies were so rotten her foot sank in to her ankle.

She and those with her removed the bodies and brought several bags of rice back to the cave. They cooked the rice under Adan palm tree on N'chara Beach and distributed it to other people at midnight.

Nunruru Cave had no fresh ground water. Seawater flowed right into it, so we couldn't do our cooking there. There was an irrigation reservoir near N'chara Beach. We used that water for drinking, cooking, and washing.

Because my mother cooked the rice and shared it, others in Nunruru Cave rushed to the storage cave to steal rice. More and more people were cooking rice on the beach.

US troops didn't come around at night, so we were all able to cook without fear. I ate my first bowl of rice in a long time, and it was extremely delicious.

look for their families so no suicide took place."

"In the cave for the Industrial Union they started killing themselves and 68 died." The cave for the Industrial Union was a shelter for people who worked for the Zamami Village government, post offices and unions. Only those families could go in. Others were rejected. In this cave, all family members were wearing their best new year's dress. They were neatly placed side by side and were lying peacefully, as if sleeping. Because 68 people were dead in a neat line, a witness said, "It's possible that a few leaders killed them one by one, put them side by side, then killed themselves."

I heard another story as well. "In a cave for teachers, Ms. Uchima and another woman were there with the principal and his wife. First, Ms. Uchima and the woman were killed by a grenade. The principal cut his wife's throat, then cut his own and died. However, he did not cut his wife's deeply enough, so she survived."

I saw the principal's wife several times after the war, but she left the island and moved to her son's house.

The father of another family in our neighborhood cut his son's throat with a razor. Next, he cut his wife's throat, but again, her injury wasn't deep enough. She survived. She always kept a cloth around her neck. I remember it was difficult to hear her speak because air leaked so badly when she talked. Her husband also failed to kill himself.

I heard yet another story. "In a cave at the foot of the mountain behind the post office, they had no grenades or razors. Two families strangled each other. The young children were all strangled. Because they didn't die quickly, as they would have with a grenade or razor, their bodies looked like they were in terrible pain."

Some people hid in a tomb in Ama. The tomb was hit by a bomb. They were buried alive.

accommodate about 100 people. Teachers, students and their parents took shelter there.

The day US troops landed on the island, Ms. Uehara, the teacher in charge in Asa, made an announcement. "In Zamami Village, office staff are going door to door instructing residents to get together at the Monument to the Loyal Dead of Maka. They will commit mass suicide."

She looked at us and said, "Are you ready to go?" I answered, "Yes!" I stood in front of Ms. Uehara with my cousin, Ai, who was a year older than me.

My mother and younger sister were there as well. Mother's eyes were wide with fear. Her face was pale. My sister looked unhappy, almost in tears. But they couldn't stop me. They just watched me quietly. That made me sad. I said, "Good bye," to my sister, and suddenly I got so scared I could hardly stay standing. I don't remember much about what happened after that. Twelve to thirteen students and their parents gathered around Ms. Uehara.

Eventually, Ms. Uehara threw a grenade to the floor with all her might. But it didn't explode. Then she took out a razor and started to sharpen it. I became terrified and ran away to Nunruru Cave, a large natural cave that could accommodate hundreds of people. It had access to the outside in various directions, so we could go in and out easily. No one was instructed to do so, but hundreds of island residents decided to take refuge in this big cave in the end.

The people in the cave had fled from different places on the island. They were talking about the mass suicides going on elsewhere.

"At Maka in Zamami Village, people got together, but many said, 'I can't do it because my family is scattered everywhere.' They went to

A kamikaze boat for use by the Kamikaze Corps was hidden in Adan palm grove near N'chara Beach, so a soldier was always watching. When we passed by, we were required to show an ID card, even if we were just going to the field.

This time, just as we were about to arrive at the mountain, a huge formation of Grumman planes flew over, and before we knew it, the entire green mountain was engulfed in a sea of fire. Students cried and screamed and ran away with no idea where to go. Teachers also ran this way and that. Somehow, I got down to N'chara Beach and hurried home. After this air raid, the mountains on Zamami, starting with Mt. Machan, burned for three days and nights.

When I got down to the beach, I saw a bonito fishing boat that was bombed in Ago Creek. The hull was badly burned. Two fishermen on the boat were killed instantly by the direct hit. The captain had serious injuries. I heard that by the time teachers got back to school, the buildings were burned to the ground.

In Asa where I lived, two houses were smashed and burned. My brother was blown through the air by a blast, but he got up and rushed to Yuhina Cave at the foot of Mt. Akazaki. All our caves were full of refugees.

The air raid went on for three days. Then, on the 26, US troops landed on our island. The Zamami Elementary School Graduation Ceremony planned for that morning at 9:00 was cancelled.

Zamami Island had three separate communities. My neighborhood was called Asa. The schools and post office were in Zamami Village, and Ama was the community on the west side of the island. Zamami Village was completely destroyed by the bombing. My family and I took refuge in Yuhina Cave where my brother was. This big cave could

When my father died, we became a family of five: grandmother, mother, myself, sister and brother.

My grandmother loved to make everything clean. She polished the floors and corridors until they shone. She hated us walking with bare feet in the house, and we were often scolded for leaving footprints.

My mother was a hard worker. She had to be to serve Grandmother. Even after her husband was gone, she made pickles from house grown vegetables, entered them in an exhibition and won first prize. I never saw her resting.

My mother went to the beach at daybreak, caught octopus and fish, and by the time when we woke up, they were prepared and ready for our breakfast. In those days, it was common to bring potatoes to school for lunch. Only a few brought rice. The school provided lunch once a week, and I looked forward to eating the creamy *tofu*.

We had to accumulate coupons to buy sneakers or clothes. It was practically impossible to buy new products, so some students came to school with no shoes at all. When the war got intense, the bronze statue of a Japanese hero was confiscated from our schoolyard by the government.

At the time of the Battle of Okinawa, I was a second-year student at Zamami Post-Elementary School. Soon after school stared in 1944, the buildings were used by the Japanese Army. They even made students scoop night soil out of the latrines they used.

We suffered a terrible air raid on Zamami Island on March 23. That day we were scheduled to go to Mt. Machan where we were going to open up some land to plant potatoes. All the students gathered at the school, walked single file to N'chara Beach in Asa and on to the mountain.

Went to mass suicide determined to die

Mie Tanaka
Born October 1930. At the time of the Battle of Okinawa. Lived in Asa, a community on Zamami Island, with grandmother, mother and younger brother and sister. The houses in the community were destroyed by an air raid. The family took shelter in a cave. On the day the US landed, her school teacher urged her to commit suicide, and she agreed. The grenade didn't explode. She felt a powerful fear and fled to a natural cave. People taking shelter there talked about mass suicide. Mother protected the family by getting rice from the Japanese Army's cave. Eighty-five years old, living on Zamami Island.

Teacher asked, "Are you ready to go?" I said "Yes!"

My huge house, located in Asa, a hamlet on Zamami Island, was built by my grandfather, who became wealthy producing salted and fermented rabbitfish, an Okinawan specialty. On rainy days when we couldn't go out to play, I played hide-and-seek with my younger brother and sister in the many rooms of our house. It was one of the largest buildings in Zamami. Sometimes during the war it was used to accommodate senior officers.

My father owned a ferryboat and was chief engineer. He died in action in China when I was in second grade. That was 1938. He was the first person from Zamami killed in the war.

That Sino-Japanese war was a war Japan won. My mother went all the way to Kagoshima to receive my father's ashes, and many people from neighboring Aka Island came to his funeral. Later, my father's name was inscribed on the Monument to the Loyal Dead of Maka. I unveiled that monument.

some of us from the line to put in another group. He took only girl students. I was one of them. After a truck ride we arrived at a hospital in Makyan. The soldiers had known we were nurses and able to help the injured.

In the truck on the way, I held the hand of a younger student, whispering to her, "When we get to the middle of the Pacific, let's throw ourselves from the deck and die, OK?" That never happened.

others would be taken as well. With my mind focused on this, I kept walking in silence.

We went out to the Mabuni Coast, but the sea there was filled with US warships. I decided to give up and said, "I can't keep going!" The others all agreed. "Rather than be caught and humiliated, we would kill ourselves."

One combed her hair. Another looked at a picture of her family. Another took her school uniform from her emergency bag and changed clothes. Each of us made our own preparations for the final journey.

Strangely, we were feeling calm. The seven or eight of us who came that far together sat in a circle. One of us pulled the pin out of the grenade and threw it hard on the ground. We competed to be the first one on the grenade. We were all thinking, "I want to be at the bottom and die in pieces." We all believed those who had told us, "If you get injured and survive, you will be sent to a comfort station in Hawaii." However, both of our grenades failed to explode.

We were at a loss wondering what to do when, suddenly, several US soldiers holding guns appeared from behind a rock. An Okinawan boy around 12 years old accompanied them. He said, "The war is over."

We attacked him. "You must be a spy for the Americans. How can you lie like that to your fellow Japanese?"

The soldiers ignored our conversation in Japanese. They pushed us forward with their guns, making us move to the direction they wanted us to go. We were taken to an open field in Mabuni. Many other refugees were there. We were forced to walk in single file to a waiting truck.

On the way an American naked from the waist up was selecting abruptly issued to the student corps. A military officer said, "You have no task here anymore. You are free to act at your own discretion!" We felt safer keeping together with as many of us as possible, but a large group would make us stand out. Our teacher said, "Make groups of four or five and break through enemy lines. Make the most of your lives." Then, she shrieked in desperation, "Don't be taken prisoner!" We had only two options: be killed by a bullet or kill ourselves.

Casualties among the Himeyuri Student Corps included 13 teachers and 123 students. Of this 123, more than 100 killed themselves within a few days after the dissolution order.

We had no idea what to do. I was "free to go" but we were in a battlefield being blasted by artillery shells. The island was full of enemy soldiers, so it was impossible to break through their lines. We went to the seashore. The west coast from Nashiro to Itoman was all beaches with no place to hide. We headed east toward Mabuni, which was filled with rocks, cliffs and caves.

We hid in the shade of rocks during the day and walked by night. By that time, I had recovered enough to walk with a cane. I did my best not to lose my friends in the darkness, while dodging the bullets that came flying in now and then.

Trudging over tremendous numbers of corpses, my shoes were completely worn out. I was walking barefoot by the time we arrived. The coral reef tore at me like a bed of needles. The soles of my feet were soon in tatters. With each step, the pain climbed through my body to my heart. Once when I had to walk on hot sand, I felt as if I were walking on burning coals. But I couldn't scream. I didn't want to let the Americans know where we were. If I were taken prisoner, the killed themselves with hand grenades. Many others crawled on the ground, crying, "Take me with you!" I knew something extraordinary was happening, but nobody told me what.

Suddenly, two younger students came flying in urging, "Let's go quick!" "Let's go, Hatsuko!"
"Where are we going?"
"It doesn't matter. Hurry up! If we don't move quick, we'll be done for."
The US troops were approaching. I walked through bursting artillery shells supported by younger students. We arrived at a place with three stretchers. Seriously injured students lay on two of them. A school teacher was supposed to be carried on the third, but her encephalopathy was so bad she resisted violently. They couldn't take her out. The teacher in charge told the younger students to put me on the stretcher. Otherwise I would have killed myself drinking potassium cyanide thinking it was medicine. I didn't know it, but my classmate had left above my head some rice, milk and potassium cyanide wrapped in a medicine paper.

I was carried toward the south on the stretcher through a storm of artillery shells. Our teacher negotiated with the leaders in several caves. "Please accept a few students." But every cave was filled with soldiers. In some cases, they threatened her with a sword.
My schoolmates took turns carrying my stretcher. My injury was only to one foot, but I still couldn't keep up with uninjured students. I felt terribly sorry to be such a burden. Finally, we arrived at the cave in Ihara on the southern tip of the Island of Okinawa.

Our stay in Ihara wasn't long. On June 18, a "dissolution order" was than a soldier." But the operation without anesthesia brought me such enormous pain, I couldn't answer him. The application of iodine was so painful it made even tough soldiers scream. The pain was like a red-hot skewer going into my wound running through my body out the top of my head. The iodine the Japanese Army used during the war in Okinawa was undiluted. Because it was filthy in the caves and wounds easily developed tetanus, we needed undiluted iodine to prevent it.

Putting myself in a tiny space as deep as I could get in Surgery Cave 24, I lay down for about ten days.

One day, I felt something strange was happening in the cave. My classmate showed up and said, "Here it is, Hatsuko. I'll be right back to take you." She put something above my head and left.

Soon I heard the sound of things falling down from the upper bunk beds. "Thud, thud." I also heard explosions of hand grenades and painful shouts of, "Please take me with you!"

Thirty-second Army Headquarters in Shuri was on the verge of collapse. The headquarters chose to withdraw to the south of Okinawa to delay the decisive battle on the mainland of Japan. They closed the Army Hospital in Haebaru. That day was my nineteenth birthday.

The Army Hospital was divided by department. The main office moved to a cave in Yamagusuku. Surgeries I and III moved to a cave in Ihara, while Surgery II moved to a cave in Itosu. Sometime later, a Himeyuri Monument was erected in Ihara.

Those who could walk were sent to new caves. Cups of milk with potassium cyanide in it or hand grenades were distributed to those who couldn't. That thudding sound I heard was the sound of patients taking potassium cyanide, dying, and falling from their beds. Some

the caves deeper and deeper. We cut and carried logs to make more beds.

On May 13, I went out to do the "meal service" and was waiting my turn behind a dry well. A few days earlier, a soldier saw my *jikatabi* (cloth shoes) and said, "If an artillery shell comes in, your foot will be blown away with shoes like that." He gave me leather military boots. They were very heavy because of all the iron hobnails.

It was not an artillery shell that got me. It was a trench mortar shell, which breaks into pieces and scatters when it hits. When it happened, I had no idea what was going on. My classmate told me later that a seven-centimeter fragment burning bright red, stuck in my left boot at the ankle. If I had not worn the boots, I would have lost my left foot. As it was, I was badly injured.

Trench mortar shell fragments are powerful enough to slash down small trees. However, when they hit Japanese fern palms, they just stick and stay. I believe this is related to the fern palm's astringency.

When a soldier gets hit by an artillery shell, chemicals often go through their blood to their brains. Then they develop encephalopathy. When that happens, they lose normal consciousness. Many soldiers suffered encephalopathy due to injuries received in the Battle of Okinawa.

To keep this from happening to me, the surgeon picked the fragment out with tweezers, then cut a big hole in my skin and the muscle around the wound with scissors and without anesthesia.

I took care of soldiers who went under amputation screaming in agony, "Kill me!" I encouraged them saying, "Aren't you a soldier of our Emperor's country?" I couldn't allow myself to scream.

The surgeon praised me. "Well, it turns out a girl student is stronger

On the other hand, maggots were part of the "maggot treatment." If they ate the pus from the wounds, the scar would heal smooth and healthy. Once a fly laid eggs in a patient's ear. There was nothing we could do. He said, "My ear hurts," and was suddenly writhing in agony. We were unable to get them out of his ear.

We had more and more patients, so the frequency of bandage changes dropped from once in three days to once in five days to once a week. Blood was rich in iron, so when it solidified, it got as heavy and hard as an iron plate. We could hardly tear the bandages off.

Some shouted in anger, "Can't you do it more gently?!" But we had so many patients we couldn't afford to take much time with each patient. I tore off a bloody-pus-hardened bandage with rotten skin and dropped it, and it made a big clang, like I had dropped an iron ball.

A soldier with a damaged brain developed encephalopathy. He lost normal consciousness and inhibitions. He trampled right on the wounds or faces of soldiers lying near him. He even urinated on the face of a soldier lying on a lower bunk.

Every time something like that happened, the victim would yell at me, "Can't you do something about him?" I was so busy day and night that I have no memory of sleeping in a bed or even going to the bathroom properly.

Everyone was dissatisfied and irritated.

All we said from morning to night was, "Yes, sir," "Please wait for just a moment," "I'll bring it soon," and "I'm sorry."

Still, they criticized us. "Okinawa's girls have no sympathy." Or "They get food and eat it all themselves." Such comments were demoralizing.

As the patients increased in number, the soldiers dug and extended

I had no doubt that the US army already knew about our hospital cave. Machine gun bullets were flying around ceaselessly, sometimes like windblown rain; artillery shells landed with a huge "boom!"

Each shell made a hole about five to six meters wide and anyone standing nearby would be blown to pieces. Mountains of earth and sand piled up around the crater. Artillery shells had terrible destructive power, so we rushed out during intervals in the firing. But machine gun bullets were constantly coming in, often hitting people. Most machine gun bullets went right through the body. The entrance wound was like a heated skewer stab wound. The exit was called a "flesh flower." A lump of flesh jumped out as if it were a blooming flower.

The stench inside the cave from feces, urine, sweat, and bloody pus was so bad it was painful to breathe. Quite a few students went out now and then to breathe clear air. Many were shot and killed.

In the cave we heard screams like, "Doctor!" "Help!" "Oh no!" and roars like, "Where's the chamber pot!" "Where's the urinal!" Those who were hospitalized were all in serious condition, often too dreadful to look at. Dealing with their feces and urine was one of our tasks.

When we first entered the cave, we had at most four or five patients. Now, we had 118. Flies immediately swarmed over the wounds and maggots multiplied rapidly. Small maggots, about five millimeters, in piles above and below, soon became fat and more than two centimeters long. One soldier injured on his back had to lie on his stomach and couldn't turn over. His back was totally covered with wriggling white maggots. We could even hear the sound of maggots eating pus from the wounds. At first, we picked them out one by one with tweezers but that didn't come close to solving the problem. We spread a shirt over the maggots and scraped them up into it, then going to the door of the cave to throw them out.

Surgery II and Surgery III. Just about all we did was provide treatment for artillery shell injuries.

I was assigned to Cave 24 in Surgery I with two younger students and one classmate. The younger students were only 15. I felt sorry seeing them carry heavy corpses and do the dangerous "meal service." My classmates and I took care of all these tasks. Passages in the narrow cave barely allowed two people to pass each other. When an injured soldier died, we lifted the body by his head and legs, placed it onto a stretcher, then carried it out of the cave. It was extremely difficult to carry out the bigger soldiers.

The "meal service" was dangerous because the kitchen was in the village of Kyan, which was two hills away. We actually risked our lives carrying rice and soup in wooden buckets through artillery fire. This "meal service" was a soldier's task in other caves, but in Cave 24, it was our responsibility. Because only students were doing it, our turns came around often.

In the rainy season, the hillside got muddy and slippery. We transported soup buckets and mess tins with rice gruel for soldiers who had difficulty eating regular food. We did our best to keep it from spilling.

In addition, the mountain path was dark, which made walking even harder. By supper time, after 7:00 pm, US troops had usually stopped firing, so that was when we went out for "meal service." The people in charge of the hospital cave came all at once, and more than a hundred duty soldiers had to wait holding buckets for meals. We left the cave at 7:00, but we would get back around 9:00. When we got back, hands reached out from bunks here and there with shouts of, "Give me some!" We pushed by those hands and went deep into the cave.

Early in the morning, around 4:00 on March 24, all boarding students were called together in the schoolground. Our instructions from the principal were, "Work as hard as you can. You are female students of the Emperor's country!" He then said, "Arrive at your destination before daybreak." We walked all the way from Higher School of Education in Naha to the Army Hospital Cave in Haebaru.

The graduation ceremony scheduled for March 25 was postponed to the 29. When it was finally held in the dim light of candles in a triangle barracks tent, we swayed at times due to the artillery shells landing nearby.

The governor of Okinawa and many other prominent figures had attended the previous year's graduation ceremony. This year, when I graduated, only the mayor of Shimajiri Village and a few senior officers from the Army attended. I received neither diploma nor teacher's license.

Haebaru Army Hospital Cave was called an Army Hospital, but any buildings out on the ground could be targeted from air or sea. The Army dug more than 30 tunnels in the mountains in Haebaru and used those as a hospital.

When we first arrived, the hospital had only a few patients. We took wooden shutters from empty houses in Haebaru, placed them on the ground and used them as beds. As soon as the US landed and invaded, the number of patients increased rapidly. Bunk beds made of logs were lined up in rows.

At first, the hospital had three departments: Surgery, Internal Medicine and Contagious Disease. After the US landed on main island of Okinawa on April 1, an increasing number of injured were sent to us from the front lines. Our departments became: Surgery I,

School of Education.

I was a boarding student. Those who skipped the preliminary course and went directly to the regular course were required to live in a dormitory. Those who graduated from girls schools tended to burst into laughter and talk more freely. We were often described as "free," meaning "uninhibited."

After 1944, the 32nd Army for Okinawa Defense was established and Japanese Army troops were stationed in Okinawa. The people of Okinawa found themselves under a Total Mobilization System; school lessons were replaced by military labor.

The Japanese Army trained nurses in preparation for the US landing on Okinawa. This training was provided by noncommissioned officers and medics in the afternoon at the auditorium. Second-year students from the Higher School of Education along with third and fourth year students from First Girls High were in nurses training.

We also went every day to Oroku with soldiers to help build the airfield there. My classmates and I were swinging pickaxes to crush hard coral rock. We put the gravel in a big colander, carried it to a depression and made bumpy ground flat for the runway. The US arrived so that airfield was never used by the Japanese army.

On March 23, 1945, a US air raid hit several islands of Okinawa. On the 24, we, boarding students, received our mobilization orders.

On March 23, 222 boarding students from the Higher School of Education and First Girls High School along with 18 teachers, a total of 240, became the Himeyuri Student Corps.

Tended injured soldiers as Himeyuri student nurse

Hatsuko Arakawa
Born May 1926. Nineteen years old and second year student at regular course in Okinawa Women's Higher School of Education at the time of the Battle of Okinawa. Received nurses training, joined Himeyuri Student Corps. Cared for injured soldiers and worked for the food service at the Army Hospital in Haebaru. An artillery shell fragment stuck in her ankle; a serious injury. The hospital had to move to a different cave. Potassium cyanide was distributed to those who couldn't walk. Fled with the help of her schoolmates, but eventually decided to join a group suicide. Found by American soldiers, sent to a hospital in Makiya. Ninety years old, living in Toyonaka City, Osaka Prefecture.

Packages of potassium cyanide placed by the injured

After the war ended, I learned that more than half of the students in the Himeyuri (star lily) Corps were dead. I felt sorry for those classmates, and I suffered for a long time from guilt over having survived.

I was originally from Kyoto. My father was a policeman and was transferred from Kyoto to Okinawa, where his parents' house was. Because of this transfer, I entered First Okinawa Prefectural Girls High School when I was a third-year student transferring from Kyoto Prefectural Momoyama Girls High School.

Two years later in 1943, I went on to the regular course at Okinawa Women's Higher School of Education. These two schools were annexed and located on the same grounds. Most students who graduated from First Okinawa Girls High went on to the Higher

there to rest.

We finally arrived at Cape Kyan but found the same scene we had left in Shuri. The main street in Kyan was full of dead women and children. US troops were already invading, and their hundreds of thousands of vehicles were moving. The bodies of the women and children were mashed by military trucks and tanks, their shredded skin scattered all around. I wondered if the bones of women and children might be weaker and easier to crush. There was no blood, no swarm of flies, maybe because the corpses were so dry and dirty. Even in war, I felt it was just too brutal not to clear away the bodies properly. They just rode right over them with their military vehicles.

The night we arrived in Kyan we slept in a small cave. The next morning as we left the cave, a large number of jeeps drove up and American soldiers piled out. They knew refugees were hidden in the caves. We were ordered to walk to an open field in Itoman with other refugees from that area.

A huge number of refugees gathered in that field. After spending a few days in the field, we were divided into groups, assigned to camps, and loaded onto trucks. My family was sent to a camp in Ishikawa.

As soon as we arrived in the camp, my mother heard her name being called. One of her students recognized her, one who had not gotten onto the Tsushima-maru. Seeing that child brought the painful memory rushing back. Mother's face contorted in agony. She almost burst into tears. She immediately turned to an officer and said, "I want to take care of these children." Many orphans were housed in that camp, and every camp had an orphanage. Because my mother went to work in the orphanage, we were separated from her until we left that camp.

bones smashed, nothing but skin and clothes remained. So many tanks and trucks passed over them that no blood remained to be seen. The first time a body was hit by a tank, it bled. But when that body had been run over again and again, the tracks and tires just carried all the blood away.

Like us, all these people had come to headquarters for protection. As soon as my grandmother saw all those dead bodies, she stood up, her body ramrod straight. She had been riding on my mother's back. As a doctor's wife, she had never gone anywhere without a rickshaw, but she started walking on her own two feet.

Shuri was completely destroyed, so we decided to head for Cape Kyan to the south. We didn't head north because a branch of our grandfather's clinic was in Motobu. In summer, my family used to visit our relatives, and we children would go swimming. We usually went by bus, leaving home early in the morning, arriving at night. The transportation system in that area was poor, so we decided it was impossible to travel all the way to the north with grandmother on foot. So we chose to go by way of Tomigusuku. I was in charge of finding food because I was healthy and physically strong. My mother had to take care of Grandmother. My sister had a lung problem and could barely walk.

Many houses were empty because their residents had fled the bombing. Some were still burning. I entered those houses being careful to avoid the fire. Most had earthenware pots holding potatoes and beans the owners had been unable to take with them. I put those potatoes and beans in a pan I found in the kitchen and put it on the smoldering ruins. Soon, the potatoes were baked and the beans were cooked. At night I would find an empty cave, and we would all go in two of us carried a large straw bag on our shoulders. We had learned at school how to offer first-aid, so we disinfected and bandaged wounds for any of our classmates and soldiers who got injured while working.

The soon-to-be famous "Himeyuri Student Nurse Corps" attached to the Army was assembled in haste. Students living in the dormitory were able to assemble early in the morning and act as a group until late at night, and did so when the war got intense. It was organized by students who had come to First Girls High from distant islands or the northern part of Okinawa. Those who lived in Naha City (like me) were not included.

Because I lived at home and not in the dormitory, I had no friends in the Himeyuri Nurse Corps. But I knew most of those who died. Many were classmates. After the war ended and our lives were a bit more settled, those of us who had attended the school from our homes participated in a class reunion. We called the names of the deceased boarding students, recalling them all, one by one.

Eventually, the air raids got so intense, my family decided to leave Kakihana. We thought if we went to Shuri, where Army headquarters were located, the many soldiers there would protect us. My grandmother, mother, older sister and I left Kakihana.

Arriving in Shuri, we were stunned. Dead bodies lay all over the steep road leading toward headquarters. Nearly all the bodies were women or children. The adult men had been drafted into the Defense Corps, so very few were there. And, I saw no Japanese soldiers. I wondered where they had all gone.

Those people had been killed by artillery fire from the ocean or bombing from the sky. Shuri Headquarters soon fell, and a huge number of US Army tanks landed on the beach, rolling right over those bodies. Human beings were crushed and tattered like rags. The

others on board, casualties exceeded 1700.

Later, when the guardians were informed regarding the incident, families who lost children thronged to our house from early in the morning to late at night. My family was trusted by these families. My grandfather was a doctor. My mother was a teacher. And because she was an experienced teacher, she made it her own job to take special care of problem students. Bad boys respectfully called her "stern teacher."

The parents had lost their beloved children so suddenly and unexpectedly. They were full of rage and grief, with nowhere to express those emotions, which is why they came to our house. They accused my mother saying, "Mrs. Makishi, we let our children go because we knew you would take care of them. You didn't go, so why did my child go without you? Why did you put our children on a boat that was likely to sink?"

Seeing their parents, the students' faces appeared to her. She called each student's name, over and over, saying, "I'm so sorry! Please forgive me!" She put her hands on the *tatami* mat and lowered her head in abject apology day after day.

At school, my mother had to encourage the young teachers, who were also being blamed by parents and were thoroughly discouraged. And yet, when she was alone, after the parents left, she sat late into the night feeling guilty about surviving. "Why am I left all alone? I can no longer afford to live thoughtlessly!" Her suffering was too painful for me to watch.

Meanwhile at Himeyuri, all students were mobilized to "assist our soldiers." We worked building gun batteries at Oroku airfield. In cloth bags labelled "working bag," we packed soil and carried it away. Or

was the most prestigious girls school in Okinawa. It was traditionally called Himeyuri (star lily). My mother had graduated from Himeyuri.

The navy blue middy blouse and skirt of the Himeyuri uniform was extremely attractive to local boys, but when I entered the school, the war was on so we had to wear a shawl-collar blouse and *monpe* work pants.

Every morning my sister and I took a Kadena line train to our schools. Mother saw us off, then left for her school. My grandmother took care of all the housework, so mother could stay late at school helping young teachers.

By August 1944, Japan's military situation was grave. Over 800 pupils in eight elementary schools in Naha City were ordered to evacuate from Okinawa to Nagasaki. My mother was to go with the students and care for them in Nagasaki. The teacher's family was allowed to evacuate with her, so after some discussion, we decided that we would all go to Nagasaki. We would rent a house there and live very much as we did in Kakihana. We sent our household goods ahead and, bringing only personal effects, went to Naha Port, where the Tsushima-maru was soon to depart.

Suddenly, a young couple, both teachers, appeared and, though not registered for evacuation, asked my mother to give them our places. The person in charge of the evacuation said, "Having two young teachers would be better to care for the children at the destination." Our family evacuation plan was cancelled.

A few days later, we learned that the Tsushima-maru was attacked by a US submarine and sunk. The incident was not announced right away to avoid harming our fighting spirit. My mother heard about the sinking from a colleague at school and was profoundly shaken. Hundreds of children died. Including parents, guardians, teachers, and

Mother in agony after her evacuating students are killed when their ship was attacked

Yoko Kamiyama
Born August 1929. Third-year student at First Okinawa Girls High School at the time of the Battle of Okinawa. Lived in Kakihana, Naha City with grandmother, mother (a teacher at the local elementary school) and an older sister, who attended Women's Higher School of Education. The parents of children killed in an attack on their evacuation ship thronged to her house to blame her mother. She hated to see her mother so unhappy. Engaged in military labor with the student corps, but as the war intensified, her family decided to flee. On the way she was shocked by the sight of masses of dead bodies crushed to pieces. The family was sent to a camp where her mother offered to take care of the camp's orphans. Eighty-seven years old; living in Naha City.

Student evacuation ship attacked and sunk; mother's students died

My father was the only son of my grandfather, who was a doctor in private practice and an Okinawa Prefectural government worker. My father fell ill and died when I was two, so I have almost no memory of him. Soon after my father, my grandfather died as well. Around the time of the Battle of Okinawa, I was living with my grandmother, mother, and older sister, who was 18. We were a female family.

My mother was a teacher for Kakihana Elementary School in Naha City. My sister graduated from First Okinawa Girls High School and went on to Women's Higher School of Education. I was a third-year student at First Okinawa Girls High. My school, founded in 1900,

"I'm hungry." But he couldn't talk so he spoke by crying.

I couldn't see any injury on his mother, but she was as thin as a skeleton. It was obvious to me that she had died of hunger. She had nothing with her. I wondered if her things had been stolen, or maybe she just didn't have anything.

People usually moved in groups, with family or friends or neighbors. It was quite unusual to see a mother and child alone like this. The boy must have been extremely hungry, but nobody else even stopped to look at him. It might be because I stopped that he cried until tears had wet his entire face. I recall his eyes, and my heart fills with unbearable pain. I wonder what happened to him. I wonder if he starved to death with his mother. I hope someone else took care of him.

I stopped and looked at him for a short time. I wanted to help him, but soon, I turned away and started walking fast to catch up to the others. I looked back again and again, but nobody even stopped to look at him. Even when I could no longer see him, I heard his long, loud cries, over and over. I hear them now.

the circumstances, it seemed best that we surrender. But my father, oldest brother and second oldest brother said, "They'll think we're soldiers, so we'll be killed." They ran deeper into the mountains.

Twelve of us turned ourselves in to be prisoners of war. We were sent to a refugee camp in Sedake. My father and two brothers ran through the mountains to Arume. Luckily, they met a friend who had come back from Hawaii and was able to speak English. My father and brothers heard from him that the rest of us were now POWs. They decided they couldn't keep running, so the four of them started walking toward the camp in Sedake. On the way, they ran into about thirty American soldiers. While they were questioning my father, the friend from Hawaii told them in English, "This man is a school principal, not a soldier." That saved my father and all four of them were taken as prisoners. They were brought by jeep to the camp in Sedake.

One scene I will never forget, and when I remember it, I feel pain in my heart even now. We were walking from my mother's parents' house to my father's parents' house in Aritsu. Just before we arrived, I suddenly heard a baby crying. The road was full of twists and bends, and the forest along it was dense, so I couldn't see far ahead. I could only hear the crying. We kept walking and there, but the side of the road, was the body by a woman in her early twenties. Her face and neck down to her chest were sunburned and very dark. By her side, a little toddler lay limply on the ground, his legs stretched out. It was a boy about a year and a half, and he was crying desperately. He may have started crying when he noticed us getting close.

His hair was wild, like the quills on a porcupine. He wore a dirty singlet. I stopped to look at him. Looking up at me he opened his eyes and mouth, writhed, and cried louder, begging for help. He grabbed his mother's *monpe* work pants to say, "Please, help my mommy!" Or

back to Aritsu.

We stayed in Aritsu for a few months. One day my oldest brother appeared unexpectedly. His unit happened to be withdrawing and, in the morning of April 26, they were passing through Arume, near my grandparents' house. My brother remembered the area, so he asked his senior officer if he could go see his grandparents. The officer gave him permission on condition that he would be back by 2pm. Seeing him in military uniform but so much thinner because he'd had hardly any food or drink for more than a week, we all cried. It was a brief reunion, and too soon, it was time to go. Grandfather knew the area well, so he offered to go with my brother and guide him back to his unit.

On the way, they encountered three American soldiers. Grandfather noticed the Americans first and sent a "get away" sign to my brother, who was walking behind him. Grandpa drew their attention and asked them to let him go because he was an innocent old man. They let him go, and he got home.

My brother found it impossible to return to his unit, so he came back to our house in Aritsu. After the encounter with the Americans, Grandpa said, "It's too dangerous here. Let's go hide in the mountains." So the whole family, 15 of us, hid deep in the mountains.

Several villagers saw the Americans and the rumors spread. Some Japanese soldiers in the village heard the rumor and decided they had to kill them. They went out looking. They found them and chased them. They shot some as they dove into the sea or tried to hide behind a rock. Three of them raised their hands to surrender, but the Japanese fired anyway and killed them.

On hearing about this incident, the US Army set all the houses in our village on fire, burning them to ashes in retaliation. We watched the whole process from up in the mountain, and were horrified. Under

parties in that room. I call them drinking parties, but no one was singing songs, talking loudly or laughing. All they did was fill each other's *sake* cups quietly. The next day, they went to fly their kamikaze missions.

People were saying that US troops were landing on Okinawa. We were forced to abandon the school and evacuate to my mother's parents' house in Mihara. At school, we had to worship the Emperor's picture enshrined in a wooden box in the indoor playground. I carried that box on my back as we headed for my grandparents' house.

My mother's parents were wealthy farmers. They had a large storehouse beside the main house to hold grain. When we arrived, dozens of people who lost their houses during the October 10 air raid were already packed in. The main house, the barn, the large workshop with its dirt floor—every room with a roof was filled with refugees. There was no space even to walk around, and more people were rushing in one after another. The food in the storehouse was gone in no time. Those coming in late were begging. "Just a potato skin, please, give me something to eat."

We decided to leave Mihara and go further north to Aritsu, where my father's parents lived. We made our way on a narrow winding mountain road with many other refugees. When we arrived in Aritsu, we learned from other refugees that my oldest brother was posted in Izumi, a section of Motobu. My mother immediately said, "I'm going to see him!" We tried to talk her out of it because it would be dangerous, but her mind was made up. So Father told me to go with her, carrying my one-year-old sister on my back.

It took days, but we arrived at last in Izumi. However, each unit was assigned a signalman, and my brother had been transferred to another unit. We were unable to see him. Terribly disappointed, we walked me shoot down that Grumman!" Everyone around him was trying to stop him saying, "If you go out there, the Grumman gunner will kill you."

I watched the October 10 air raid from our residence on the school ground. Countless enemy planes flew across the sky, not only over the southern area where the Japanese headquarters were but Awa in Nago City and the whole northern part of Okinawa, but they didn't attack us. The enemy planes were flying slowly and in formation. The Japanese fighters and anti-aircraft guns fought back.

After the October 10 air raid, my mother took my little brother and sister and evacuated to her parents' house in Mihara near Kanucha Bay. Father had to stay to protect the school. My thirteen-year-old brother and I stayed with Father. My oldest brother was drafted as a signalman at age sixteen. We didn't even know where he was. Soon after the raid, even my thirteen-year-old brother received notice from his school that he was drafted into the "Iron Blood Student Corps for the Emperor." He left for the Corps with two cups of rice in his socks.

He later told me that the drafted students assembled in Isagawa, Nago City, and each was given two grenades. Just when he had made his peace with dying for the Emperor, he was told, "First- and second-year students, you are dismissed!" He never went to the battlefield.

Our elementary school was commandeered by the Army. The kitchen next to our residence was used as a barracks kitchen. The military cooks delivered rice and miso soup in buckets every morning, noon and evening.

In a detached room of our residence, an eight *tatami*-mat room was prepared for newly-appointed teachers. After the Army came, seven or eight kamikaze pilots were always around and often had drinking wearing white long sleeve aprons peeled the stems and dried them. They smelled good. Some people think the taste is too strong, but I think they make a tasty side dish.

Our school had lots of straw men for military drills. We were told to imagine that they were enemy soldiers and stab them with bamboo spears. The female teachers had to be especially serious about this.

We carved our bamboo spears on the slant to a sharp point. We put lard on the tip and roasted it in a fire, making it almost as strong as a metal spearhead. The boys competed to see who could make the strongest bamboo spear.

The bucket brigade for firefighting is now a fond memory. The anchor would pour water in the bucket, which was then sent hand by hand to the fire. We were taught a special technique. They told us that unless the water arrived all at once with our total physical strength, it would have no effect.

Okinawan schools in those days were subject to another education policy. "The use of the Okinawan dialect is prohibited." Anyone who spoke in our native dialect was forced to hang a card around his or her neck saying, "I will speak standard Japanese."

One day before October 10, I was walking in a potato field carrying my brother on my back. Suddenly, out of nowhere, a US plane appeared and flew very low and very close to me. I quickly ran to a depression in the field. Turning back, I clearly saw the face of the soldier in the cockpit. I often remember that day. It's a kind of trauma because I know I could easily have been shot and killed right then and there.

I went straight back to the shelter and found a big argument going on. A Japanese soldier in the shelter had a gun and was shouting, "Let

servile, but a degree of poverty makes people pure and sharp."

I have almost no memory of playing with my older brothers. Since I was the oldest daughter, I carried my three-year-old brother on my back and went to play on Katsudake Hill with some friends. My oldest brother was accepted by one of Okinawa's best schools, Third Okinawa Prefectural Junior High School. The school was far from our house, so he got a room at our paternal grandparents' house, but soon, at the age of 16, he was drafted to serve as a signalman.

In front of our elementary school, we had a shelter for each grade and one for teachers and staff, so we had a total of seven shelters. Students in the third grade and up dug those shelters. They were pits, like octopus traps. They looked like shelters, but without a roof, everyone inside was visible from above.

When we had evacuation drills, a whistle would sound, then a big drum would start beating. At that point, I had to run for our fourth-grade shelter. I had to rush into the shelter before the drumming stopped. If I failed to get to the shelter in time, I had to lie face down on the spot where I was when the drumming stopped. That's why the front of my *kimono* was always muddy. I didn't wear shoes. I was always barefoot.

As the war situation worsened, Japanese soldiers were stationed in my school. Soon, we had two military guardsmen standing continually in front of our school gate. Everyone in third grade and higher went out to pick Japanese silverleaf, which we gave to the soldiers to eat.

We put a massive amount of Japanese silverleaf in a rope basket. It was a huge basked we used for "agriculture class." Eight of us carried it—two on each side, two in front and two behind. We would carry the basket into the school. Then, Women's Association members

A baby crying desperately by its dead mother

Reiko Kajiwara
Born November 1933. Eleven years old at the time of the Battle of Okinawa. Lived in the principal's residence on the grounds of Awa Elementary School with parents and five siblings. Family fled to her mother's parents' house in Mihara, but the large number of refugees already there made them go on to her father's parents' house in Aritsu. On the way she saw a baby crying by its mother, who had starved to death. Everybody was completely focused on how to survive. It was impossible to save the baby. The baby's cry remains deep and indelible in her mind. Now living in Naha City, eighty-two years old.

An American plane came so close I could see the pilot's face

I was eleven, in the fourth grade at the time of the Battle of Okinawa. My father became principal of Awa Elementary School in 1943, so my family moved to Awa, Nago City. My family was eight people; my parents, oldest brother (16), second oldest brother (13), me (oldest daughter, 11), younger sister (6), younger brother (3), and youngest sister (1).

We lived in the principal's residence on the school grounds. We could go back and forth between our house and school through a corridor. But when I went to school in the morning, I had to go out the school gate, meet my team, and when all the teams had gathered, walk to school through the school gate led by the sixth graders. We had to walk to school in groups.

My father was a very serious person. He neither drank nor smoked, and he lacked flexibility. It seems he was the kind of principal the school staff tried to avoid. He often said, "Dire poverty makes people

Now and then, I still see a young girl and remember Keiko and Toshiko playing on the beach, bursting into shrieks of delight.

The old man's wife held him until she was stabbed in the chest several times by that short sword. The old couple fell to the ground, bloody all over and eventually stopped moving. Crouching behind a bush, watching this whole process from beginning to end, I urinated involuntarily.

The Battle of Okinawa ended a month later. Those who had been in big caves were sent to refugee camps. A Japanese manager sent by the US military came to our small cave and said, "We are building more camps but with so many displaced, there's no space for you. Go back to your village for now." So we did. Two or three houses were burned out by air raids, but ours was intact.

Fifty to sixty villagers came back, and the rumor was, "We've been abandoned. American soldiers will come and kill us all." Meanwhile, malaria was spreading through the village. Another rumor was, "The US army is spreading malaria." I was terrified.

One day my mother began to tremble with a high fever. She had malaria. My grandmother was next. We had no medicine. There was no thermometer in the whole village. My shivering mother seemed resigned to her fate. "Your grandma and I have a contagious disease. Don't come close to us. Be careful!" She and grandmother went into the furthest room and never came out.

My mother went first; grandmother went a few days later. Because the crematory had been destroyed by an air raid, relatives came quickly and buried them in the family tomb. The malaria outbreak reduced our village population by half. Mitsuko and I were left alone.

Still, we had our house and farm. I had farmed with my mother since I was very young, so I knew how to grow vegetables. That was a big help. My sister and I worked together to plow our field and grow a lot of potatoes, which we sold in markets. That's how we lived.

side of the cave. The blast collapsed the cave and buried me. Several villagers rushed to dig me out. I was unconscious for three days, lying in a corner of the cave.

Going back to my main story, when mother, grandmother, Mitsuko, and I finally reached the caves on Mt. Motobu Fuji, they were full of soldiers. My mother begged them to let us in, but we got no response until a man who looked like a senior officer lifted a stick to chase us away.

To prepare for the landing of US troops, villagers made caves for their families and Japanese soldiers dug caves for themselves. Villagers, who knew the land thoroughly, found strong ground to dig into. Soldiers would dig randomly. When they found the soil too soft and prone to collapse, they stopped digging and began to search elsewhere. There were quite a few incomplete caves started by our troops; we ended up in one of those shallow caves.

While we were going back and forth between the cave and our tomb, I got malaria. My fever climbed over 40 degrees. I shivered all over and was only vaguely conscious. Soon I was too weak to move.

Then my mother shouted, "Put something in your mouth! You'll die if you don't eat!" and beat me with a stick. It was so painful I desperately ate potato, millet, anything she gave me. Thanks to my mother, I got the physical strength I needed to escape death.

We stayed in that cave for a while. One day I went to the latrine and heard some US soldiers' voices. I quickly hid in an Adan palm grove. Hand in hand, an agitated old couple came out of a shabby shelter at the foot of the mountain. Suddenly one of the soldiers shouted something, pulled out a short sword from his waist and cut the old man's neck. His head dangled down, and the soldier rapidly turned red from the gushing blood.

you to go." However, Keiko and Toshiko were so frightened by the shooting from the warships, they refused to move. "I don't want to go anywhere. I want to stay here with my father."

Suddenly, we heard a dog barking. Mother quickly hid the two girls in the tomb and closed the door. We left and began rushing through the brush in the woods. I was holding my grandmother's hand. Suddenly, we heard fierce barking from near our tomb, then gunfire that went on and on. We knew immediately that my sisters had been shot. My mother and grandmother squatted and cried for a while, but soon we ran away, sobbing.

The next day, we waited till the bombs and gunfire stopped. We went back to our tomb. Two girls with bobbed hair lay dead on top of each other. They were probably holding each other in fear when they were shot. We were afraid the enemy might come back, so we didn't even bury them. We put a rush mat on top of them and returned to the cave. Four or five days later, we were able to bury them.

I experienced the death of other relatives as well. It happened around the time of the "Okinawa Blitzkrieg" on October 10, 1944. That time as well, we were in a cave near the village, one dug by our army. There were stable private caves here and there near the frontline, but my family was not allowed to go in them.

My uncle knew that, and I think he felt sorry for us. When he was on cooking duty, he came to give us some rations. He was saying, "Hey, I have some food for you. Please—" when a bomb killed him.

When that bomb hit the ground, it made a big hole four or five meters across. The bowls and other utensils he brought were scattered all around, along with pieces of his body. Our relatives gathered the parts of his body, put them in a box, and buried them in a tomb.

I heard about this. I didn't see it because I was in a tunnel in the

My sisters and I were always together. We played on the beach in front of our house when I could take time away from housework. My mother made us all swimsuits out of old clothes.

Because the ocean got deep so gradually, when the tide was in, Mitsuko and I swam offshore. We dug in the sand with our toes to catch white clams. When the tide was out, we caught fish that failed to ride the ebb tide and struggled in pools between rocks. We grabbed them by hand. Keiko and Toshiko were small, so they played in the sand. When we went home my mother would have made soup with white clams and broiled fish, so we would sit down to a tasty dinner.

When the battle started, our village was destroyed by artillery fire from the ocean or bombs dropped from airplanes. When we heard that US forces would land on Okinawa, we couldn't dig our own "family cave" because our whole family was female. In fear and helplessness, we decided to hide in our ancestral family tomb on a hill about ten minutes on foot from our house.

In Okinawa, we have Buddhist memorial services called *Shimi* in spring and *Higan* in autumn. Families carry feasts to family tombs and spend time with ancestors and deceased family members. We often visited our family tomb and felt easy being with our father. The room in the tomb was big enough for all six of us, so we hid there and kept quiet.

After a while, a policeman from the village came to tell us, "The US has landed. It's too dangerous here so go on into the mountains." He made this suggestion because the Japanese army had dug some large, stable caves on the side of Mt. Motobu Fuji, some 10 kilometers away.

At first, my mother insisted on staying at the tomb but the policeman was adamant. He said, "You have children and an elderly woman here. If you stay you'll be killed. I got permission for all of

My two younger sisters were shot in the family tomb

Hiroko Kakazu
Born July 1933. At the time of the Battle of Okinawa, 11 years old and living with her mother, grandmother and three sisters in Shinzato, Motobu Village. As artillery fire from battleships and air raids gained intensity, six family members took shelter in the family tomb on a hill. Later, the family was told to take shelter in a cave, but two younger sisters stayed at the tomb and were gunned to death. Becoming bedridden with malaria, Hiroko slipped in and out of consciousness, but miraculously recovered. After the battle, her mother and grandmother both died of malaria. Hiroko and her remaining sister cultivated and sold vegetables, surviving by helping each other. Now eighty-three, she resides in Ginowan City, Okinawa.

Our family of women couldn't dig our cave

Shinzato community was a quiet, rural settlement at the tip of Motobu Peninsula. The villagers grew sugarcane, potato, millet, and spinach beets. Spinach beets are a big leafy vegetable with white stems that we stir-fried or boiled. We also fed it to our pigs. The shallow ocean near our house had made the beautiful white sand beach that stretched far out in front.

My father fell ill and died when I was seven (four years before the war ended). I lived with my mother, grandmother (father's mother) and three sisters.

I was eleven at the time of the Battle of Okinawa. My sister Mitsuko was eight, Keiko was five and Toshiko was four. As the oldest daughter, I helped my mother and grandmother with housekeeping and farming.

After a while, our family was allowed to go home to Ufudo Village. Our house and mountain were burned by a flamethrower. Even the ground around it was charred. By the time we finished building a hut on the mountain, my father had malaria. He had a high fever and was shivering all over. I took him to a clinic. This "clinic" was at the extreme far end of our village. It was nothing but a converted pigsty and had no medicine. My father died in November 1945.

I was left alone with my mother. We had no farm to produce crops. We had no income. We had no food in our hut. Soon, my mother was bedridden from malnutrition. Every now and then I went out for "military gains." We called it "military gains" but it meant stealing potatoes from somebody else's field. I pulled potatoes with the runners and shared them with Mother. We ate potatoes, potato leaf, runners and everything. It was a time when food was in extremely short supply, so if I had been found, I would have been killed for sure. But I would do anything to eat. During that time of my life, I was so desperate I remember almost nothing about how I survived.

My mother grew weaker and weaker. One morning in 1948, I woke up and she was cold. Her last words, spoken in weak voice, remain in my ears. "We have no food, so I can't keep going."

an open space in the village. From there we were made to walk in a stream all the way to Imadomari.

I kept my personal belongings in a wooden pail on my head. I was walking along with my parents. Suddenly one of American soldiers knocked my pail down from my head. He was using gestures to say something like, "Putting something on your head won't make taller." But I was so scared I couldn't pick my pail up. I kept walking silently.

We spent a night in Imadomari. The next day, we were taken in a truck to a refugee camp in Oura in Kunigami.

In the camp it often happened that young women were raped, killed and thrown into the jungle by American soldiers. People whispered, "That girl hasn't come back" or "Another one's gone." Another rumor was that quite a few girls were raped but didn't make any noise. They just kept quiet and lived.

In Oura camp we were provided meals but only a small rice ball once a day. Everybody was always hungry, so young women went out to look for food in the potato field. That's when they were taken.

I went out looking for something to eat with my cousin Chiyo, who was two years younger. When we came to a place where the mountain slope rose to the left, and a roaring river ran on the right. Suddenly I heard a rustling sound. I looked left toward the mountain. Two black soldiers jumped out of the brush. These soldiers were running toward us at a tremendous speed. Their eyes were bloodshot and it was obvious they were going to rape us.

In an instant, I thought, "We'll be raped and killed!" Shouting "Mommy" I grabbed Chiyo's hand, and dove into the roaring river. I would have dived into fire, if necessary. I was that scared. The two of us got back to camp dripping wet and in tears.

the school building was empty. Rumor had it they had all been sent to Ie Island. During the war, everything was secret. If you even tried casually to find out something, you were suspected to be a spy. So I never knew where they went.

Eventually we heard a rumor that the US had landed on Okinawa. We thought it would be dangerous to stay in our home, so my parents and I hid in a small natural cave in the mountains. At night we went home and made rice balls and other food, which we packed in our lunchboxes. We brought them back to the cave and ate there.

One night when we got back to the cave, we found it smashed to pieces by a bomb. It seems a reconnaissance plane had seen us coming in and out during the day. We would have been killed instantly if we had been in the cave. We found another cave and hid there, but we were scared every day.

After the US invaded the Island of Okinawa, American soldiers with guns came searching through the mountains right near our cave. As soon as we heard voices, the gunfire sounded. I saw people with their arms blown away. Others were shot in the side. The injured people screamed and ran out of their caves.

We couldn't look at them, even when we heard their screams. We were silent and motionless, like stones. We waited quietly for the Americans to leave. Thinking that bullets would fly into our cave at any moment, we were frozen with fear.

We spent days in the cave not knowing that the war had ended. American soldiers brought Japanese-American interpreters, who called to us in Japanese saying, "Please come out. Please come out."

Villagers who had been hiding in caves came out from here and there. My parents and I, too, went out. We were all called together into dig lots of pits called Octopus Traps on Mt. Yae. Then, when the US troops landed near Nago and moved inland, Japanese soldiers would be hiding in the pits and shoot them. My task was to dig those holes. We built two mountain shacks, one for male workers, the other for female workers. I slept in a huddle of about twenty women in the female shack.

Digging octopus traps was extremely hard work. We had to dig out tree roots and throw them down the hill into the valley. The work was all done on a steep slope, so if someone above us dropped a root and we failed to dodge it, we could suffer serious injury.

One day, just as a yellow alert sounded, a US plane flew over and fired its machine gun. People ran in all directions. Watching carefully to avoid being noticed by the enemy plane, I ran at full speed along a road for eight kilometers. I simply fled back to my house. I don't know how many people were killed on Mt. Yae that day, but I never went back to that workplace and the project was abandoned.

In the village, every time rations were distributed, I went to the rationing center about one kilometer from my house to get food for the family. There was a school building near the rationing center. Everyone said it was used as a dormitory for fighting units. Some young men looked out the windows, so we saw each other whenever I walked by. After a while, we knew each other's faces. But we had never talked so I didn't know their names. Every now and then I heard some of them loudly singing military songs like "Farewell Okinawa…"

One day, I went to the rationing center and a clerk gave me a package of cigarettes. "A soldier in the fighting unit told me to give this to you." That reminded me of some young men who came to buy cigarettes at the rationing center. I thought one of them must have given me those cigarettes, but I had no way of knowing who. Soon,

My first military job was to cook for Japanese soldiers living in more than 70 houses in our village. One whole house was assigned to be the kitchen, and women cooked the meals there. Soldiers came to get the food in buckets three times a day.

After that I was sent to build an airfield on Ie Island. We were told to build "the number one airport in the East," but our working conditions were terrible. We had no house so we slept in a big tomb that held the ashes of all the members of one large clan. Japanese soldiers put all the ashes together in a corner without permission and made twenty or more female workers sleep in the tomb. There were many such clan tombs in the area.

We had no mats or anything to put on the floor, so we just lay down on the ground wearing our *monpe* working pants. I was so miserable I slept sobbing, "Mommy, Mommy." I was youngest in this workplace, too.

The men with pickaxes would loosen the dirt, and we female workers would put that dirt in a wheelbarrow and carry it away. I was on Ie Island over a month, returning to Motobu Port on April 1, 1944.

As soon as we arrived at the port, an air raid started. Enemy planes flew down low, fired machine guns or dropped bombs. A lot of people were killed. I threw myself down on my stomach on the sand and rolled under some trees. I barely survived, but I did make it back to Ufudo Village.

Ufudo was in a valley surrounded by jungle. Trees grew high so airplanes couldn't fly very low. The mountain roads were nestled in the trees so it was difficult to see people from the air. Many people who lost their houses in the October 10 air raid took refuge in Ufudo.

My third military job was constructing a fort on Mt. Yae. From the top of Mt. Yae, we could see the whole town of Nago. The plan was to

Knowing we were about to be raped, my cousin and I dove into a raging river

Katsue Yonamine
Born August 1929. Lived in Ufudo, Motobu with her parents and helped support the family by working with her father since elementary school. In place of her elderly father and physically weak mother, she was drafted into military service. She endured hard labor but ran home when the US started bombing. In the refugee camp, she had a horrible experience. Her father died of malaria. She tried desperately to get food for her mother, but she, too, passed away from malnutrition. Eighty-six years old, resides in Naha City.

Drafted to military service, I sobbed every night because of the hard work and loneliness

I was born in Naha to an already elderly father and sickly mother. My father's job was making washtubs. He was a heavy drinker, which was hard on our family finances. We moved to Ufudo on the Motobu Peninsula hoping life would get easier.

I would put the washtubs my father made on my head and take them to town of Motobu to sell them. That was our only income. Because I was working in this way, I had to drop out halfway through sixth grade. Father remarried my mother, and I'm their only child.

When the war got intense, one person in each household was drafted to military service. My father was too old; my mother was weak, so I had to go for my family and work with adults. I was the youngest in every workplace I was assigned. But the bosses never took my age into consideration. They never gave me light work. They always yelled at me saying, "Why can't you do it faster?!"

they still weren't back. I was afraid something bad had happened to them. I couldn't sleep at all. I just waited for dawn.

I have never been more relieved in my life than I was when, just at daybreak, I saw them coming back with big smiles on their faces. My brother was carrying a big bag of rice. Mother was carrying other food on her head.

early one evening as soon as the artillery fire stopped. Before we had made any significant progress, we ran into a young American soldier. When I saw him with a rifle hanging from his shoulder, I felt as if my heart would stop. I thought if I looked at his eyes he would kill me, so I kept looking down. My grandpa put hands together and spoke in desperation. "Please, these are my grandchildren. They are only women and children. Please let us go. Please."

I don't think he understood what my grandpa was saying, but it might have been too much trouble to take us to a refugee camp. Or maybe he just felt pity for us because we were so weak and shabby. Acting like he didn't see us, he nodded and left.

When we arrived at my uncle's house in Shimoda near Tamagusuku Hyakuna, the house was filled with people who had fled from Naha or Shuri. We went straight to a stable and secured our space.

One day I saw in the distance a long procession of refugees led by American soldiers. They were probably going to a camp. Others at the house were saying, "Wherever they're going, they'll all be killed." Hearing this, I was again deeply grateful to the soldier we encountered who let us go.

I think it was in September. We had hardly any food so we were eating potato vines, when we heard a rumor. "There's food in caves that people have run from."

My brother and mother wanted to try the hospital cave in Itokazu. But we had also heard that some had stayed there, people who went there for food were killed. But my grandparents and little brother and sister were so hungry they were just lying around listlessly. Eventually, my brother and mother decided to go to the hospital cave.

I was terribly fearful and restless. They were gone for hours, and of the shelling from the ships was too intense. We lived our entire lives in the cave, from cooking for over fifty people to defecating, which caused the air to smell terrible. We lived like that for about a month. One day we learned that US tanks were coming toward us at an incredible speed from Cape Kyan. We waited for night, then moved in the rain to a cave near the ruins of Tamagusuku Castle.

I will never forget that move. The whole area was covered with mountains of corpses piled here and there. I lost my straw sandals and was walking barefoot. I went forward through the darkness with bare feet stepping on corpses. It was too dark to see, but sometimes I felt I was stepping on a baby's face, or its mother's. I can still clearly remember the feeling that came up through the soles of my feet when I stepped on the side of a flabby body.

Many of the things I saw or heard have faded with time, but the memories of touch never vanish from my mind. The smell of rotten corpses that filled my nose step after step, and the sickening splash of body fluid on my feet. I hated all of that, but I couldn't stop. If there is a hell on this earth, that is the time and the place. And yet, I did nothing more than feel the sensations. I ignored them because I had to escape.

My brother and mother kept bringing us edible things, like wild grass or tree buds. Staying alive on those things, we stayed for a long time in the cave at the ruins of Tamagusuku Castle. The *kimono* I wore was dirty with rain and mud. Nothing of its original form was left. I was dressed in rags.

Before long we thought, "We can't stay here forever." We decided to go to my grandpa's relative's house in Shimoda. We left the cave a little butchered their horse, which they ate for some time. Others, saying they had found a safer place, ignored their orders and left the cave.

Nobuo worked hard and did his best to keep us alive. In fact, we all survived thanks to his tremendous efforts.

It was rainy season and water fell drop by drop from the roof of our cave. We took off our clothes and squeezed them, wiped our bodies dry with them, then we put them on again and dried them with the heat from our bodies. This was the best we could do to keep dry.

My sister Tsuruko got something like diaper rash. The area around her anus got swollen and red. She couldn't take a bath and her seat was always wet so that area got inflamed and developed a skin disease. She gradually got weaker and weaker. She was always crying and saying in a feeble voice, "I'm cold. I'm cold."

In addition to potatoes and other food items, my mother often groped around in the darkness and found mugwort. She boiled it and applied it like a poultice on Tsuruko's seat. Tsuruko complained about the pain, but that was the only treatment we could give her.

The cave was pitch dark at night. We couldn't identify anything without touching it. My little brother and sister trembled in fear, and I would hold them. I think they knew they were in a dangerous situation. They trembled but they never cried or shouted out loud.

As I looked at the ocean, I often saw kamikaze airplanes with the Rising Sun emblem fly right into a US warship. Most of those kamikaze planes exploded like fireworks and fell into the ocean before they could get to the US ships. It was so pathetic and infuriating, I shuddered.

We couldn't take even a step out of the cave during the day because carried a few cooking utensils. My grandparents held the hands of my little brother and sister. We walked all the way to the cave in the pouring rain.

Grandfather said, "Since it's raining this hard, they probably won't fire on us today." Right after that, they attacked us in a heavy downpour. Fragments of bombs and mud flew everywhere. Those fragments hit many of us. Quite a number of people lost hands or feet or were killed. A fragment hit my grandpa's forehead, and his face was quickly covered in blood. A fragment stuck into my back, causing me to run frantically in pain and fear. That fragment remains in my back today.

When an artillery shell is fired, we hear a low thumping sound. The shell flies through the air with a whistling sound, and explodes with a tremendous boom when it hits. I felt the most fear when I heard the explosion.

The white coral reef out in the clean, beautiful blue ocean of my childhood was suddenly covered by US warships. The oil coming out of the ships dyed the ocean black.

We had no soldiers in the natural cave at the fork in the road. We had only 50 to 60 neighbors. Each family had to get its own food. Collecting food for eight family members, including my grandparents and little brother and sister, was a heavy burden for Nobuo. When the artillery fire stopped at night, Nobuo got Mother to go out with him to look for food. He was 15, only a few years older than me, but he looked very much like an adult man.

One time he came back near dawn with tiny leftover potatoes from a potato field that farmers had finished harvesting. We all eagerly shared that meager fare. One family led by an adult man is said to have was on a boat that was hit and sunk in the October 10 air raid just off of Kume Island. We never received his body.

This incident was reported under the headline "Over 600 civilians drafted from the Island of Okinawa killed."

I remember my father fondly. I was his first daughter so he cared for me with great affection. He took me everywhere he went. The year I entered elementary school he took me on a train to Naha. Train rides were rare in those days.

We lost our father, and fifteen-year-old first son Nobuo suddenly became the head of the family. He had to take care of us. My school recommended me for temporary evacuation, but my mother was against it. "Without her father, she shouldn't live separately from the family."

One day, my uncle, who was usually on Kume Island building an airfield, came to our house to say, "The US army has landed on Okinawa." About that time, Tamagusuku was being hit with artillery fire from just offshore. We fled behind a big rock near the house. My aunt, who was living next door, didn't flee with us for some reason. Soon, she was blown away by a bomb that threw her body up into a Malayan banyan tree. She was rather small and sweet.

Like many other houses, our house had a thatched roof. A single shell blew away more than half the house. The community chief came to give us instructions. "You're assigned to the natural cave at the fork in the road." In those days we couldn't even choose our own refuge. The village chief gave us an order, and we had to go to the designated cave. The natural cave at the fork in the road was quite far away.

It was rainy season. My brother Nobuo took the lead. My mother

Okinawa 1944-1945

Running away on decomposing bodies

Shizuko Maehara
Born May 1932. At the time of the Battle of Okinawa, she lived in Tamagusuku, Nanjo City, with her grandparents, mother and siblings. When her father was killed in the October 10 air raid, her family took shelter in a natural cave and lived with other refugees. Her older brother, 15, supported the family, getting food with her mother. When the family was moving to another place of refuge, they encountered an American soldier. Grandfather begged desperately to be let go, and the soldier left. The family encouraged each other and survived together. Now 84, living in Yonabaru, Shimajiri County.

My father's boat was sunk during the October 10 air raid; his body never came home

At the time of the Battle of Okinawa, my family was my grandparents, my mother, my siblings and me. My older brother, Nobuo, was 15, I was the oldest daughter at 13. My younger sister Tsuruko was 9, then I had a five-year-old brother and a three-year-old sister.

My parents were farmers. Two of my father's brothers lived nearby. The three families helped each other planting rice, digging potatoes, pressing sugarcane, and with other farm tasks.

The ocean was right in front of our house so we often went to Oh Island to gather shellfish. On the hill behind our house stood the ruins of Tamagusuku Castle, or the Amatsugi Castle when Okinawa was still the Ryukyu Kingdom. I often played in a large marsh near the ruins with my younger sisters and brother, and my friends.

My father was conscripted to build an airfield in Yaeyama in 1944. He

turns explaining that the war was over. They played the radio broadcast of the Emperor's announcement through a speaker and made us listen to it.

We believed it. The next day, responding to their call, at around two in the afternoon, all of the refugees in the cave went out to be taken prisoner. I think about a hundred of us surrendered.

For all practical purposes, the Battle of Okinawa ended on June 23 with the suicide of Commander Mitsuru Ushijima. Not knowing the war had ended, Mieko had continued fleeing here and there for more than a hundred days.

A lot of American soldiers gathered to see us. Yuki was a year younger than me. She and I had gotten close while in the cave, and we were the only female prisoners. The two of us, side by side, simply walked into the middle of a flood of camera flashes.

We kept walking in the dark until we arrived at Cape Kyan. On the beach, sharp-pointed stones stuck through the soles of my *jikatabi*. It was so painful I could hardly walk. We found a large number of people already there. The beach was jammed with a crowd like a festival.

Maybe because of malnutrition, they seemed to have no strength. As the tide came in, quite a few people were washed away by waves without saying a thing. I wonder how many days we walked after that. Avoiding the day, we headed north at night. We walked along a railroad track, and when we got near Yonabaru, someone got caught in some barbed wire. Flares shot up with a boom, and bullets flew everywhere.

I panicked and tried to get away. A Korean refugee was shot and fell down on me. His buttocks were on my face, and I couldn't move.

He groaned in agony and was shouting something in Korean language. Aiming at his voice, American soldiers fired at close range. Since a flare was up, if I were to move I would be shot as well. They shot him, and he was dead. When his groaning stopped, the bullets stopped coming toward us at last, but the firing continued for over an hour.

Just before dawn, I crawled out from under the corpse to find I was alone. Later, when the battle was over, I found my husband, Nae and Hide.

In the area around Maeda in Urasoe, I was surrounded by a large number of people, remnants of the defeated army and refugees. It seems the war had ended some time earlier, and they were just roaming around in a crowd. I joined them.

This was sometime in October. One evening, a few second-generation Japanese Americans visited the cave where I was hiding. They took

The three of us held a hand grenade in front of us and pulled the pin out, but it didn't blow up. Maybe it was wet because of the long rain we just had. We tried hard to make it work, but it wouldn't blow up. We threw it on a stone as a last resort, but it still didn't work.

We were alive, so we kept going. Until we got to Arakaki we were mostly able to eat cooked food. After that, we ate raw plants we found in the jungle. We couldn't find water so we couldn't wash what we ate. We rubbed the leaves with our hands, then ate them. This is an indelicate part of this story, but one day I noticed when I defecated that living maggots swarmed out of my anus. I must have eaten leaves with fly eggs on them. They incubated and grew in my stomach. Could that have happened? Or maybe I drank water from the pond with dead bodies floating in it. Were the eggs in that water? Seeing that those maggots had not been killed by the acid in my stomach, I felt fear for the state of my stomach. I also developed a maggot phobia.

Later, some American soldiers carrying guns came looking for us as we hid in the jungle. We sensed the soldiers nearby. The four of us ran separately, lying down next to decomposing bodies. We stopped breathing and pretended to be dead. Flies swarmed around the corpses, fluid leaked out of them, and they smelled terrible. The soldiers didn't come near the corpses. They simply poked bodies with the tips of their guns to see if they were dead.

A few days after that, the US military sprayed gasoline from an airplane and burned the jungle we were in. We escaped the fire and decided to head for Cape Kyan that night. But once we started to walk, we noticed a long line of refugees walking in a line behind us. I wondered where they came from. They were all silent.

On the way, I saw a baby about eight months old sucking his dead mother's breast on the left side of the road. Her face and neck were infested with maggots already. It was pitiful to see her arms and legs so fresh and normal where they came out of her summer *kimono*. The sight was so pathetic, I stopped and watched for a while.

As a midwife, I cared about that baby. At any other time, I would have held him and taken him with me. But it never even occurred to me. I was only thinking that maybe tomorrow I would be dead like his mother.

We reached Kuniyoshi at last, but US soldiers were already everywhere. We discussed what to do and decided that the elders and children should become prisoners of war. They were four adults, including our eldest uncle and Aunt Ume. And there were the six children. Grand uncle took off his dirty loincloth and tied it to a branch of a tree. He held it high as ten of them started to walk toward US army tent.

It was five o'clock. The artillery fire from the ships had stopped but it was still light. Just before they reached the US tents, Japanese soldiers hidden behind trees or rocks, started shooting at them. They shot at elderly and children because they were about to surrender.

I wanted to scream "Stop it!" But I couldn't make a sound. Wholeheartedly praying, I watched over them. Fortunately, no bullets reached them.

Left behind, Nae, Hide, my husband and I decided to blow ourselves up rather than be killed by American soldiers. However, Hide was not actually our relative, so we thought we didn't have to take her with us. Hide happened to be on vacation and happened to be visiting our house when the battle started and kept her from going home.

scattered all around us. Shocking things would happen all of a sudden while we were chatting, but I just watched it all as if it were the normal course of events. I had an outrageously cool-minded attitude. Humane feelings like shock or sadness never came up. What came up at times like that was, "I want to die right now so I won't have to suffer."

I saw about a thousand refugees in Arakaki, but most of them were dead. Dead bodies were covered in maggots. It was mysterious. When a bullet hit someone, before it was covered with flies, white maggots were crawling out of the corpse. It seemed to happen immediately. It was so strange I thought, "I wonder if they put maggots in their bullets."

The area was full of corpses. Refugees were running this way and that. Some tried to get to the ocean. Others ran toward the mountains. Refugees wandering in battlefields strode over dead bodies or pushed them aside with their feet.

There was no well in Arakaki. There was a small pond, so we went there to drink. Several corpses with bloated stomachs bobbed up and down in the pond. There was no choice so adults had to give in and drink that water. For small children, parents had them drink their urine.

From Arakaki we headed for Kuniyoshi. On the way, we saw corpses piled one on another for nearly two kilometers. We didn't have the strength to push them aside. All we could do was move forward stepping on those decomposing bodies. I feel disgusted stepping on a dead rat now, but at that time, I had no sense of disgust. We wore thin *jikatabi* (cloth shoes) but I felt nothing. My mind was simply focused on going forward. I was not really human.

The instant we reached the octopus trap, a bomb fell near the cave entrance. Everyone inside the cave was buried alive. Having no tools to dig with, my husband and I ran around looking for help. Several Japanese soldiers on that mountain rushed through flying bullets to dig our family out, one by one. But Tsuru, who was deep inside the cave, was dead. She was the most beautiful woman in my big family. We dug a hole near the cave and buried her there.

The cave was destroyed by the bomb, so we headed for Tamagusuku. We walked all the night and reached Oyakebaru.

We looked like beggars. Refugees were everywhere in Oyakebaru, with more than a hundred injured and many obviously dead. We separated into groups of two or three and hid behind fences or under trees near broken houses during the day. When night fell, we walked staying close together. I hardly slept at all during those days, at least I don't remember sleeping. We arrived in Arakaki after two days.

Something very frightening happened in Arakaki. Some boys from a neighboring village were attending agriculture and forestry school. I didn't know their names, but I knew their faces. I met the youngest one by chance. He was a first-year student and wore a school uniform. He also wore a combat cap on his close-cropped head.

He said "How are you doing?" I was about to say, "Where's your field assignment? You have to hide. It's too dangerous here." But before I could finish, an artillery shell hit nearby, and he was hit by a fragment about the size of the palm of my hand.

It cut right through his neck. His head went flying, and the fragment stuck into a banyan tree very near us. The body that had just lost its head while talking face-to-face with me went into convulsions. It stayed standing for a while, then fell down on its back.

In those days I was mentally quite abnormal. Dead bodies were

blood. Even after boiling the rice, the smell of blood remained.

We spent 20 days or so in Haebaru Village. One day, in the midst of intense gunfire, a man about 35 years old rushed into our cave looking desperate. "I heard there's a nurse here. My wife's about to have a baby."

Others in the cave tried to stop me. "It's too dangerous. You can't go out now." But I ran out of the cave saying, "Babies can't wait to be born. Bullets can't hit me today!"

I had some medical supplies like scissors, gauze and a surgical knife that I had been using in midwifery school. I had brought them with me all this way, and now they were useful.

There was no hot water or cloth in the cave where the pregnant woman was. I took off my outer blouse, spread it on the weeds and had her lie there to give birth. I cut the umbilical cord and pulled out the placenta. We had no water to clean the baby, so I used the sleeve of my blouse and wiped the blood off the baby's face. He was an energetic boy, and I was truly happy when I heard his first cry.

The couple was overjoyed. In tears, they gave me a piece of dried bonito as a token of their gratitude. That dried bonito saved us from starvation later on.

We arrived at Kochinda after walking for two days from Haebaru. After about 20 days in Kochinda, I was sitting at the entrance to our cave and felt a strange uneasiness. I took my husband's hand and crawled into an octopus trap nearby.

In those days, the Japanese army had a strategy called Octopus Trap Operations. It was a kamikaze attack in which soldiers hid in a pit in the ground, and when US troop came by they jumped out holding bombs. They exploded themselves as well as the enemy troops. There was an octopus trap near our cave.

for potatoes, kidney beans, or anything we could eat. But the US battleships destroyed trees and plants, blowing them up by the roots, leaving bare ground. Wanting at least to feed the children, we desperately searched for anything at all edible.

Walking by a big pond, I saw the body of a pregnant woman in her thirties. She had probably been shot when she came to the pond to drink. I had just gotten married, so it was a particularly painful sight for me. Her upper body was naked, and her swollen belly was exposed. I took off my jacket and put it on her and her baby. I put stones on the edges to keep it from flying away. At that point, I still had the ability to mourn the dead.

We stayed in Ikeda for a few days but bombs rained down from air, warships fired from the ocean and, tank guns blasted us from the land. We headed for Haebaru Village, as if being driven by US troops.

We could move from place to place during the night because artillery fired only during the day. The children were so scared, they shivered, but if we made a sound, bullets would fly over us. Even the two-year-old knew not to cry. He walked in silence.

Shells from warships came in with a hard scream. Tank guns sounded heavy. Bombs from airplanes made no sound coming down but when they hit the ground, they burst with an enormous boom. When traveling a long distance, a rifle bullet makes a whizzing sound. When it arrives nearby, it hardly produces any sound, but it is frightening just the same.

All around Haebaru Village, on every road we took, we saw dead bodies. Since we had no food, we took rice from the dead. We felt guilty, though, and apologized. We needed water to cook the rice. Every pond or river had corpses floating in it, and the water smelled of

Then, again, the sound—pssh, pssh, getting more frequent.

My sister-in-law screamed, "Oh, my god! Americans!" The three of us dropped the big pot and ran away.

I didn't know it at the time, but a lot of enemy soldiers were sitting on the cliff over the cave where my family was hiding.

We went back to our cave taking care not to be seen by the enemy. We told the others we should leave the cave right away. If we made a sound or stood up, the enemy soldiers would find us. Under cover of darkness, we crawled one by one, from old to young, out the cave. All of a sudden, we were in the middle of a battle.

Our second uncle was crawling right in front of me, then suddenly stopped moving after a pssh sound. They saw and shot him when he rose up just a little. He died immediately without making a sound.

When I joined the Izumikawa family feeling lonely and anxious, he was the first person who spoke to me. "Your hair is so smooth and beautiful." I felt comfortable with him and trusted him. But I didn't have time to grieve his death. I left the cave silently praying that he would be happy in the spirit world. Because a family member had just been killed, we were all terrified.

We walked all night from Onaga, arriving in Ikeda in the middle of the night. It seemed refugees had made fires in the caves. Dim light filtered out here and there through the trees.

Because we were a big family of fifteen, no cave could accommodate all of us together. We separated our children into small groups and asked for them to be housed in different caves. The adults hid under trees or by the river.

Every day the artillery fire from ships stopped around five in the evening. When it did, we went to smashed farm houses looking

beautiful and elegant.

When I married into the Izumikawa family, their first son and second son were living in the family mansion. The first son had a family, so my position was "second son's wife in the first son's household." All the men in the family were off at war except the eldest uncle and his younger brother. The rest were all women and children. There were six children in the family when I arrived. The youngest was two years old. He wore a T-shirt and shorts; his close-cropped hair was pretty. This image of him has remained with me all these years.

Artillery fire from ships offshore became quite intense. My husband was a student learning to be a youth instructor in a school run by the Department of Agriculture and Forestry. He also had to attend classes to prepare for military service. I was preparing to send him out to military service. However, he was never given a military assignment. Instead, he escaped to the cave with the rest of us. In this cave, we were sixteen people in two households.

In the morning about two weeks after the US troops landed on Okinawa (on April 1) we killed a goat. We cooked it at home, which took until late that afternoon. Nae, Hide, and I were carrying a big goat pot to the cave where our family had taken refuge. We walked down toward the cave, which was below and to the left of our house on the same hill. We saw soldiers standing above our cave. It was getting dark, and it looked like those soldiers were waving to us.

I yelled "Hey! We cooked a goat pot! Come down here and eat it!" Then I heard a strange sound—pssh, pssh, pssh—three times at my feet.

"Look! Did they throw something? It looked like a signal, didn't it?"

It was too dark to identify faces. Still we kept calling, "Hey!"

our work force! We need more soldiers. Get married early and have children!"

I met my husband, Kansei because I was renting a room in his uncle's house. He was four years older than me, and his uncle asked me to join the Kansei family. In Okinawa in those days, girls often got married at 15 or 16. I was considered late at 17.

My parents were farmers. Our house was in Takahara, Koza (now, Okinawa City). My mother died when I was 14. My husband's mother was also dead. Because of the war, we had no wedding ceremony. We just held the engagement ceremony.

It was six kilometers from Onaga in Nishihara Village, where my husband's house was, to Takahara. Since his father was away at war, his eldest uncle brought the betrothal money. His three aunts put the feast into buckets on their heads and walked to my parents' house.

My father and younger sister from my side (my brothers were living in a school dormitory) and the uncle and three aunts from my husband's side (Izumikawa) attended. The ceremony was carried out with eight people, including my husband and myself.

We called it an engagement ceremony, but all we did was: my husband and I sat before small tables and exchanged cups of *sake*. An older friend of mine living in my neighborhood taught me the proper way to do it the day before. I wore *monpe* work pants. My husband wore his military uniform. My husband sat next to me during the ceremony, but I was so shy I couldn't look at his face.

The ceremony took about two hours. After that I joined the Izumikawa family and walked the six kilometers to Onaga. Izumikawa was a *samurai* family that had guarded the Shuri fortress. (Note: Shuri was the capital of Ryukyu Kingdom (1429-1879), which was taken by Japan and designated Okinawa Prefecture in 1879). Maybe because of this, the men were all gentle and kind, and the women were all

Okinawa 1944-1945

A young man I knew got his head blown off in front of my eyes

Mieko Izumikawa
Born January 1928. A student in a midwifery school, she married at 17 in 1945. As a newlywed went to live in Onaga, Nishihara Village. Sixteen family members took refuge in a cave when bombardment by ships became intense. Some family members were killed in the attack; others escaped to Haebaru, Arakaki, then to Cape Kyan. The battle ended, but they didn't know it. They kept running from place to place with other refugees. Currently living in Urasoe City, 88 years old.

Delivering a baby in a cave

I lived in a rented room in Naha where I was attending a midwifery school run by an obstetrics and gynecology clinic three kilometers away. I happened to be at a friend's house in Kadena, a town 20 kilometers north of Naha, on October 10, 1944.

My friend and I hurriedly took refuge in a cave because of an air-raid warning at daybreak. I saw the sky full of enemy planes. Though I didn't hear any sound, bombs started exploding like fireworks. Soon, the sky over Naha turned bright red, like a flaming sunset. The beauty of that sky burned into my eyes. The Okinawa Blitzkrieg started on October 10.

It was ten days before I could go back to my room to get my clothes. Almost all the houses in the neighborhood were burned out, but somehow my room was intact.

The following year, I got married at age 17. I was pressured to marry because of a national policy. "Give birth to more babies! Increase

Japanese soldier jumped the boy to take his mess tin. The boy resisted with all his might. The soldier beat and kicked him, and took the tin. Everyone was using all their energy to escape. Nobody could help that boy.

We found shelter in a cave in Cape Kyan. A few days after we got there, American soldiers came to the entrance of the cave and called, "Come out! Come out!" in Japanese. We had been told, "If they get women, they'll rape and kill you." So we smeared our faces with soot from the bottom of a pan and pretended to be boys.

An injured Japanese soldier in the cave started to yell, "We'll never surrender. Kill us all with a hand grenade." My father said, "You can't decide for the rest of us!" He used the towel around his waist as a white flag. "We'll be all right. Follow me!" He took the lead and walked out of the cave. About ten people from the cave followed him, and we all became prisoners of war. Later, we were sent from Kyan to a bigger camp in Ishikawa.

"The Tree that Listens to Weeping" still stands near a rotary in Itoman. Every time I see that tree, it reminds me of my best friend, Miyo, with blue cross stripes on her *kimono*, her long hair hanging down, nursing her baby.

One evening when we were in the Gate to a Grave, Miyo's son lost his temper and started to cry. He cried louder and louder. When a baby cried, the mother had to take the baby out of shelter. People had even heard of soldiers killing babies that wouldn't stop crying in a cave. If Isao had cried for a long time, I would have left the cave, too.

Holding her baby, Miyo sat down under a big tree about five meters from the cave. Because the shelter was called Gate to a Grave, locals called that big tree "The Tree that Listens to Weeping." When Miyo sat down at the base of that tree, she bared her breast and started to nurse her crying baby. The baby calmed down a little but suddenly, he started crying again, loudly and frantically.

Surprised, I looked out and saw her with a fragment from a bomb sticking out of her forehead. Blood was running down her face. She was killed instantly. It happened so fast I don't think her baby had time to get any milk at all.

Enemy planes flew over one after the next. I wondered if they could see Miyo's death from the sky. Miyo's mother-in-law ran out of the shelter and brought her body back. Her sister-in-law, who was in the fourth grade, carried the baby on her back as we left the shelter.

The enemy attack was so intense that all we could do was flee, each on our own trying to get away. Later, I heard Miyo's poor baby died. He slipped off his aunt's back because the shoulder straps were too loose.

As we fled, bombs fell close to me three times. Every time, I thought "This is it!" But they didn't explode, so I escaped death. I passed a boy in the fifth or sixth grade. He was running around calling loudly for his mother. She might have been killed. Seeing a mess tin hanging from the boy's neck and assuming there was food in it, a

top layer. We stayed on the second layer. A lot of ashes were scattered on the floor so we put straw mats down and slept right on them and the ashes.

That shelter housed fourteen people from three families: my parents' family, my in-laws, and Miyo Oshiro's in-laws. Miyo Oshiro was a classmate and my best friend in Itoman Elementary School. Her house was near mine so we were always together going to and from school. Miyo was lively, cheerful, and easy to get along with.

That was before Japan knew anything about volleyball, but our female teacher told us about this new ball game and taught us the rules. We used newspaper and made a fairly round ball. We wrapped it in cloth and made what we called a volleyball. We tossed it and practiced hitting it. We didn't know this game at all so nobody showed interest. Miyo was the first to say, "Yeah, I want to do it!" So I joined the team, as well. Miyo was the leader.

A teacher in charge of discipline criticized us. "You're playing a game from an enemy country!" But Miyo and I didn't care. We said, "It's alright because we play it after school!"

As soon as I got married, I introduced my husband's nephew to Miyo, and the two of them got married. She took our family name, Oshiro, so we had the same name. She had a baby boy in no time. Miyo's baby was eight months and mine was a year old when we got together in the shelter. We talked about our babies and what our husbands were doing. Miyo's husband was drafted and employed by the local Defense Corps. He moved around Okinawa building airfields.

In those days, supplementary foods like condensed milk and milk cakes were distributed for babies through the rationing system. She and I exchanged information about food and always asked, "How much food does your baby have left?"

take me back to his house. My family made a new set of futon and a new kimono of Okinawan fabric. I took them with me when we married.

Because of the war, we didn't have anything like a "wedding reception." About 30 friends and neighbors came over, so we made plenty of bean sprout salad and served it in shell flower leaves, which we ate in the yard.

The house I married into was in our neighborhood so I would just show up at my parents' house. My father scolded me. "No matter how close you live, once you marry, you shouldn't visit your parents so casually."

The following year I gave birth to my first son, Isao. I was 18. Then, on the 18th day after his birth, my husband, who was in Navy, boarded a destroyer and left for the front. My husband's family included his parents and their forth son, who was a student. I was busy taking care of my newborn.

Grumman bombers flew over constantly and started bombing us. We decided to take shelter in a cave in Kakazu. We waited for night, then hurried to the cave with my mother carrying Isao on her back. I put a bucket of food on my head. My father carried a spade on his shoulder. The spade was to bury a body if someone was killed.

Sometimes they shot flares into the air. A bomber would fly over using that light to take aim. If they saw people going in and out of a building or cave, they would bomb that target. We felt in danger at the cave in Kakazu, so we went further down to a cave in Teruya. But soon the cave in Teruya was targeted. We finally took refuge in a shelter called "Gate to a Grave" in Itoman. It was a huge tomb turned into a shelter. It was a three-story structure. It had stairs, and the graves were on the

My best friend killed by a bomb under "The Tree that Listens to Weeping"

Ume Oshiro
Born July 1926; youngest of eight siblings in Itoman. Married at 17; gave birth to her first son the next year. Introduced her best friend to her husband's nephew, and they got married. Took refuge in a shelter in Itoman with her best friend's family but her friend was killed by a bomb. Fled through intense air raid; became prisoner of war, sent to a camp in Ishikawa. Ninety-years old, living in Itoman City.

When her baby cried, the mother had to leave the cave

I was the youngest of eight. The others were all boys, so I was the first daughter of the Uehara family. You might think that being the first girl I got special care, but you would be wrong. My father was stern and strict. I was never allowed to go out at night. The only pleasures of my youth came after I married.

As a child, I was always running around barefoot on the beach. That beach was so clean and beautiful, I never stepped on anything that hurt me. I got married at seventeen. My father scared me saying, "If you don't marry now, you'll be mobilized to a munitions factory in the main islands of Japan." I took him seriously. In those days anyone could be drafted anytime into the war effort.

The man who became my husband was ten years older than me and lived in my neighborhood. We knew him, and my father liked him so much that he asked him to marry me. Our wedding was carried out in the neighborhood according to Okinawan tradition. Several people holding lanterns came from the groom's house to meet the bride and

My mother lost her husband so suddenly. Taking her three children, she fled desperately from place to place with a large group seeking refuge. We hid in the bushes during the day and moved at night. I vaguely remember walking along the beach in Itoman. We pressed our bodies close to a bank above the beach when a large number of vehicles full of US soldiers went by. However, we were eventually caught by US soldiers near the beach and were taken prisoner. When I saw half-naked soldiers having fun playing catch or basketball on the base, the gap between our situations was too much for me. My fear dissolved into astonishment. I just kept thinking, "What is going on? What has all this fighting been about?"

At one point, they put us children together and handed us each cookies right out of a can. I can still remember how tasty they were. Later we were sent to a small village and given a shack to live in. Each family lived in a shack and cultivated a field. We lived there for a several months.

When the war ended, my mother went back to her brother's house in Oroku. She immediately got some relatives to go back with her to where my father lay. She remembered the name of the village and the house. To be sure she could find his remains, she had buried him in a crater near the corner of the main house. When we arrived, red hibiscus flowers were in full bloom, as if they'd been waiting to greet us.

a very bad feeling about him going out, and soon we heard the roar of bomb exploding nearby. Mother was instantly worried about Father. She ran out and found him face down on the ground. He had been killed instantly. The soldier was already gone.

Mother pulled Father into a crater near the house opened by another bomb. She couldn't bear to put earth directly on his face, so she covered it with a towel, then buried him. As she did, some Japanese soldiers just watched her with a grin from the other side of the crater. When telling this part of the story, my mother always shook with anger saying, "I hated them enough I would've killed them if I could've."

Mother finished burying father all by herself, then told him, "I'll come back to get you when the war ends. Please wait for me here till then." She broke off a bunch of hibiscus branches and planted them around where he was so she could find him.

My father's sudden death was terribly painful for me as well. He was a rickshaw man, He was cheerful, fun, and a good father. I was his first daughter, and he loved to make me happy. When he went to pick up a customer in the red light district, he often took me with him riding on his rickshaw. My mother told me I was very precocious. Once, when we arrived at a brothel, I started dancing to the music, imitating the *geisha*.

My father knew I had no interest in dolls. He bought me lipstick and face powder, like the *geisha* wore. Those were my treasures.

Another memory I have of my father was going to Oroku riding on his shoulders. We got to a farm and he picked a bunch of Japanese lantern plants for me. He picked so many I could barely hold them in my arms.

A Japanese soldier jumped out of a nearby cave and shouted, "Hey! Bring that girl here!" We had lost track of my father and brother. Mother was carrying my younger sister on her back and pulling me by the hand. She later told me she thought that soldier would kill us.

It was taken for granted in those days that you obeyed any soldier's order. My mother said she resigned herself to our fate and pulled me into the cave. She couldn't stop trembling in fear, but the soldier said, "Lie her down on the table." She had no doubt he would kill us, but instead, he pulled the bomb fragment out of my forehead. He sterilized the wound and even applied some ointment.

When he pulled the fragment out, the blood gushed out, but he pressed hard on the wound and stopped the bleeding. Then, he wrapped a bandage around my head many times and fastened it tight. My mother said me it was easy to find me in crowds after that because of the bandage on my head. This bandage stayed on until I was treated by Americans as a prisoner of war. The wound never got infected. I have always wondered if that soldier was an army surgeon or medic or just an ordinary soldier. I have no way of knowing who he was, but he saved my life.

My mother, my sister and I kept moving, looking for safe place. We found my father and brother completely by accident at the entrance to a village. My mother burst into tears of joy. Feeling so much safer, we took shelter in a farmhouse.

The next morning, right after we were all together again, a Japanese soldier jumped into the house with a gun in his hand. He pointed the gun at my father and said, "Go out there and see where the enemy troops are coming from!"

Father was probably thinking, "He'll kill us all if I don't do what he says." So he went out without a word. My mother later told me she had bullets flying this way and that.

We walked along a country road for several days. We carried no food or water. Once when I got thirsty, my mother found a reservoir and gave me water from her hands. I was happy to drink, unaware of anything else. I heard later that the reservoir was full of corpses, some floating, some at the bottom.

Finally we got to a farmhouse in Itoman. Several other families were already in that house, and the adults in each family huddled together to sleep. But we children were running around everywhere, not really staying with our parents. I'm sure there were more than twenty children.

A few days later, my father and older brother were cooling themselves in the evening breeze out in the yard. Suddenly, a bomb fell on the house. Mother, still carrying my sister on her back, searched frantically for me in the dense smoke.

She pulled children out one by one shouting, "This one is not Sumiko! This one isn't either!" I remember her screaming my name as she dug desperately to save me. This is actually a good memory for me.

As soon as she found me, she pulled me out and we left the crushed house. We took a few steps, turned back, and the house burst into roaring flames. My mother saved me at the last minute. Many of the children who had been playing with me were killed.

I remember a street in Itoman crowded with the people flowing in from every corner of town. A bomb dropped in the middle of the crowd, killing many of them. A fragment from that bomb hit the left side of my forehead just at the hairline. I ran screaming with pain and fear through a street full of bloody people and dead bodies. Mother chased me and took my hand.

Okinawa 1944-1945

Ordered out of the house by a Japanese soldier, my father obeyed and was killed by a bomb

Sumiko Tokuyama
Born October 1939. Five years old at the time of the Battle of Okinawa. Lived in Naha with parents, older brother and younger sister. Beloved by her father, a rickshaw man. She remembers him taking her along and putting her on his shoulders. Seriously injured by a bomb fragment, but lived because a Japanese soldier treated the wound. When the family took shelter in a farmhouse, a Japanese soldier came in, pointed a gun at her father and ordered him to go out an observe. Father went out and was killed by a bomb. Mother buried him by herself and planted hibiscus around his grave. Seventy-six years old, living in Okinawa City.

I heard my mother screaming my name

I was only five years old at the time, bit I can talk with confidence about the Battle of Okinawa because my mother often told me about it in great detail. It was how she remembered my father. In a sense, my testimony is both mine and my mother's. Her name was Kame Gushiken.

Before the battle, my family lived in Wakasa, Naha City. Every morning, I saw the food unit carrying breakfast in big containers. I saw them from a window and cheered loudly, calling out, "Soup unit!" or "Rice unit!"

My family was my father, my mother, my brother (10), my sister (1), and me (5). When the war came to Okinawa, Father took us to Itoman, in the southern part of our main island. We fled through

I turned to my mother and said, "I'll come back to get you. I'll take you home. Please wait. I'll be back, for sure." Then, we gave in and were taken prisoner, leaving my mother still breathing in the cave. That was June 23.

The refugee camp was located in Sashiki. As soon as I could, I went back to the cave to get my mother, but she was gone. I have no idea what happened to her.

That was a year of terribly sad and bitter experiences. The only bright spot was, as my mother said, the smiling face of my son, who was going to turn two soon. He had no understanding of the cruelty we had suffered, so he was quick with his beautiful smile. Our family felt his smile was giving us the hope and desire to live.

I have many memories of my mother. I was closest to her of all my eleven siblings. My parents were rich, but they had many children and many migrant farmers coming in and out. She was always busy. Naturally, I was in charge of serving tea to the migrant workers. It was also my task to clean every room before I left for school each morning. My mother watched me and often said, "My life would be so hard without you."

Often when I came home from school, she was mashing soybeans to make Okinawan *tofu*. It was always fun to help her.

When I went into sixth grade, Mother told me, "Nobu, I want you to go to junior high." But thinking about my brothers and sisters, especially the twins, I answered, "It doesn't matter about me. I want to be with you, Mom."

I loved my mother so much, my greatest happiness was to be with her as much as possible.

with fair-skin and big round eyes. He was always singing. My father loved Shigezo and gave him a horse. Collecting grass for the horse was his main chore. He was always humming and cutting grass.

He had gone into our house to get a drink of water. When he came out, a soldier shot him. Maybe he was angry at Shigezo because he wouldn't stop singing, or maybe he did it just for fun, but he took a rifle and just shot Shigezo in the stomach.

I couldn't stand to see him pressing his stomach, rolling around, struggling in agony in the farm. We all wanted to go to him but we couldn't. An enemy plane was right above us. Shigezo was suffering and screaming loudly, so the soldier thought he would attract the enemy plane. He kept firing at my brother to quiet him. He finally did. It was all just too cruel. I was stunned and just sat there holding my son.

Watching Shigezo being killed, my oldest brother couldn't vent his anger at the soldier, so he took a sickle out and shouted insanely, "No one in my family will be taken prisoner! I would rather cut their throats and kill myself!" He thrashed violently. I used all my strength to hold him down as he raised the sickle over his head.

I wondered if he thought Shigezo was killed because the soldier thought he was a spy. Or maybe he wanted to think that and just exploded in anger. My brother was completely out of control, furious with nowhere to vent his rage, but he calmed down during the night.

Immediately after Shigezo was killed, a US tank arrived. We were called out of the cave. I tried to tell them with gestures that my mother had tetanus and was here in the cave, but I couldn't tell if they understood me.

An American soldier ordered, "Hurry up and get in the truck!" I told my brother, "I want to stay here with Mother." But he shouted, "You'll be killed if you stay! Come on, let's go, quick."

Saying, "If I'm going to die, I want to die on my farm!" my father dug another hole near a Japanese installation right next to our farm. We all moved in.

Wherever we were, we were hungry. To feed my younger brother and twin sisters who were still growing and had big appetites, I carried my son on my back and went to rather distant farms looking for potatoes and sugarcane. While I was out, a shell fell on the installation. My father was holding my sister, Teruko, and was standing just outside the hole because it was too hot inside the hole. They were killed instantly by the blast. My mother was seriously injured by a fragment that hit her in her neck.

My younger brother, Shigezo, was taking a nap in the hole and had no injury. People nearby buried father and Teruko on the farm.

The hole near the fort was too dangerous, so we abandoned this hole when we found an empty cave on the hill in the back of our house. My mother's neck, shoulder and arm were painfully red and swollen, with maggots crawling around the wounds. But we had no medicine or anything to put on it. All we could do was to pick the maggots off.

After a while, my brother, who had been discharged from the Defense Corps, finally found us. He said, "If the Americans come, we'll be run over by tanks. It's too dangerous here. We have to get out right away."

My mother's wounds were festering from her neck down her arm. I cried and begged him. "I can't go without mother!"

But mother gasped, "You have a sweet baby, Nobu! Go and live for your boy. Go to some safe place, and go now! Don't worry about me!"

Just then, I heard the sound of gunfire and my brother, Shigezo, was shouting. "Ow, ow, ow, help me!" He had contracted meningitis when he was five and was slightly mentally retarded. But he was a lovely boy

We picked potatoes and put them in a pile. We were about to pick leeks, cabbage and other vegetables, but as soon as we started to move, a warship from Nashiro Beach started shelling us. This was long before dawn. We had no chance to get the potatoes. Just as we started to run, a shell hit right behind us. Knocked down by the blast, we lay there as earth, sand, and stones rained down on us. I thought, "I'm finished!" But I got up and started running again. Another shell hit 20 meters in front of me. I threw myself down on my stomach in panic and escaped injury. We dodged shells all the way back to the cave.

After that, we stopped going out, even at night. My father went out to dig potatoes and get the food. I stayed in the cave and polished brown rice. One day a Japanese soldier came to our cave and said, "The Army is going to use this cave. You have to leave." We had lost our house. Now we were being driven from a cave. We had nowhere to go. Those who were evicted with us just moved here and there around that area. Some were hit by bullet or bombs and were killed. Others were hit but didn't die. They rolled around in agony. It was terrible. Dead bodies lay all over the place, rotting and stinking badly.

My father took the seven of us home. When we arrived, a senior officer yelled, "Why are you doing back here?!" My father did his best to make a fierce look and yelled back, "This is my house!!" Maybe surprised by his furious response, the officer ended up saying, "You can stay a few days until you find somewhere else."

Inside, the house was completely different from the house we lived in. Injured soldiers lay all over, even in the kitchen. There was nowhere to step. Using a pickax and shovel, father dug a hole near the house and we moved in there. Soon a soldier came and said, "There's nothing you can do here. We're the ones fighting!" He forced us out again. They probably didn't want to see us.

of bombs. I thought "Something is strange." The army broadcast a message. "These are enemy planes. Find a safe refuge!"

I was shocked and ran into a cave with the other people from our village. This cave was a large natural limestone cave with an underground river and connections to the "east cave", "center cave" and "west cave." Evening came and no more airplanes could be seen, so we went back to our village. The village had been attacked and turned to burnt ruins. Of over 30 houses in the village, my house and very few others were still standing.

My house was a new two-story building. It was distinguished by its two chimneys and was admired by the other villagers. A few days after the October 10 raid, a Japanese force burst into our house and said, "The army will be using this house as of today!" We were driven out.

The war was going badly for Japan. My older brother was drafted into the National Defense Corps by the Island Residents Mobilization Act. My sister was eighteen. Drafted as a nurse by the Mountain Division, she was killed in action.

My oldest brother's wife and two older sisters led our younger brothers to Kunigami. They evacuated leaving seven of us behind— my parents, a younger brother, Shigezo, who was 19, my twin sisters, Teruko and Miyoko, my baby and me.

We rested in the hot, humid cave during the day because if we went out, an enemy plane would attack us. When night fell, we cooked rice or went out to dig potatoes and find other food. Artillery fire seemed to attack Shuri continually, late into the night, not only in the daytime.

One night around three in the morning, I went with two friends to our family farm to dig potatoes. We could usually hear shells being fired even in the middle of the night, but I remember that night was eerily quiet.

Okinawa 1944-1945

I gave in, became a prisoner, and left my dying mother in a cave

Nobu Tamashiro
Born November 1920 to a rich farm family in Uegusuku, Itoman; lived with parents and ten siblings. She was 24 at the time of the Battle of Okinawa. Losing her husband, she returned to her parents' house with her son. After the October 10 air raid, the family was driven out of the house by the Japanese army and took shelter in a cave. Then, was driven out of the cave. Father and younger sister were killed by an artillery shell. Mother got injured and contracted tetanus. Younger brother was shot and killed by a Japanese soldier. Other family members were taken prisoner by the US and put in a camp. The smiling face of her baby was her only hope. Ninety-five years old, living in Itoman City.

My brother, shot by a Japanese soldier, died rolling in agony

My parents had a large farmhouse in Uegusuku, Itoman. They cultivated sugarcane, potatoes and a wide variety of vegetables. In spring many migrant workers from Kunigami came to help with the planting.

My parents had five sons and six daughters. I was the third daughter. I got married at 21 and soon gave birth to a boy. Not before long my child turned one, my husband got food poisoning from eating goat stew and died. When he was dying, he said, "After I die, go back to your parents' house and raise our child." So I went back to my parents' house in Uegusuku with my son. My son and I made my parents' house lively, reminding me of the old days before I got married.

I clearly remember the air raid on October 10, 1944. A large number of airplanes filled the sky and flew calmly, so I was watching them thinking they were Japanese planes. Then they dropped lots

this way. This way of thinking brought me this far.

off, I saw a lot of maggots in the wound where my arm had been, but the wound gradually got better. Then, a doctor decided to give me another operation to get rid of a bone that was sticking out. My arm was removed right up to the shoulder.

I will never forget August 15. American soldiers were shooting their guns all morning. Japanese patients who could walk were hiding. I was sure the Japanese army had come back and was fighting. But when I came back from where I was hiding, the Japanese were all crying. I asked why. They said, "Japan lost the war." I pulled a sheet over my head and cried. August 15, the end of Japan's war.

Later I learned what happened to my friends. Shige, who remained in the cave, died there. Kazu, with whom I went out of the cave, contracted tetanus after separating from me. She also died. Fumi and Nobu were found by US troops and became POWs. They died from sickness, but quite a while later.

I heard my younger sister was in Ishikawa. She was the only one in my family who survived. I went to see her. She burst into tears when she saw me without a left arm. She told me how my parents, two older sisters and their children were killed.

I couldn't go out of the house. I was afraid to be seen. My body was too disfigured. When I saw young women put on makeup and go out to work at a US base, I couldn't help feeling miserable. But I summoned all my courage and tried to think, "I shouldn't care too much about how I look." A relative got me a job at a distribution center.

Things got better when I started thinking, "I lost my arm to war, not by nature." I apologize. I know this seems like an insult to those who are actually born disabled, but it was just too hard to live without thinking

Then Kazu said, "It's just your arm. You can walk. Let's get out of here!" We waited for night, and four of us left the cave. We left Shige behind.

My bleeding wasn't completely stopped. After a while, I was unable to walk anymore. I couldn't even sit up. My throat was so dry I thought it was burning. At daybreak, I thought, "I'll drink a lot of water and die." I left my friends and crawled to the river in the cave. Several corpses reduced to skeletons were lying there, but I didn't think anything of it.

I cleared the surface and scooped water from deeper in the river. I drank as much as my stomach would hold. I carefully washed my arms and feet, filthy from living in caves for more than three months. I went up to the bank feeling refreshed.

Suddenly, I heard words I couldn't understand. I turned and found several American soldiers coming toward me. They were pointing at me. I hadn't been able to walk, but I was terrified. I stood up and ran about ten meters. Then other Americans were in front of me.

Surrounded, I just sat down. They tried to make me understand using gestures and signs. I think they were saying something like, "We'll take care of you." But I was sure they were going to rape me. I just shook my head no.

One of them picked me up gently and put me in a jeep. I didn't feel alive. I just kept trembling. Arriving at a refugee camp, I was surprised to see more than a hundred refugees there.

The Americans immediately operated on me in a field hospital. My left arm was rotten, all black and full of maggots. They cut it off. I was in shock for a while. For days I kept screaming, "Let me die! Kill me!" People treated me like I was insane.

About a week after the operation, I was moved to a hospital in Ginoza. I got my first change of bandage. When the bandage came

Around June 20 the Army issued a dissolution order saying, "US tanks crossed over the mountain."

The Battle of Okinawa ended with the suicide of Commander Mitsuru Ushijima on June 23.

The soldiers left our cave, and only five of us remained. Even the monitors were gone. We talked and finally agreed, saying, "Rather than going out of the cave to be killed separately, let's die together here." The next day, every time a bomb hit the mountain, the cave shook tremendously. Soil and stones fell from the ceiling. We resigned ourselves to being buried alive. We lay a wooden door on the ground and sat on it holding each other. We sat that way for a few days. We had no food. We placed mess tin covers in several places to collect water dripping from the ceiling. We put the water together and shared it to relieve our thirst.

The firing continued for a long time. One day, one of the shells flew into the cave. All I remember is my mind being numb. I lost consciousness. When I came to, I felt my left arm was too heavy. I saw it was bleeding badly. Trying to stop the bleeding, I put my arm above my head and grasped the wound with my right hand. In the darkness, Fumi put on a headlamp, took my leather belt from my waist, and tied it tight above the wound.

Fumi, too, was injured—her leg. Shige was hit by a pea-sized shell fragment that stuck right between her eyes. She was unable to sit up. I was sure she would die.

If we stayed, sooner or later the enemy would come. I told my friends, "You go. I'll stay here with Shige."

was extremely painful. There was no anesthesia available, so the surgeon amputated injured hands and feet without it. Other soldiers held down the injured, who screamed, struggled, and cried out loud. Senior officers yelled, "Hey! Is this how a soldier acts!?" Officers would slap soldiers in the face until they lost consciousness.

It was rainy season, and the situation in the cave became even more gruesome with mud and maggots swarming around in blood eating amputated limbs. The skin between our toes festered.

Just when we arrived at the cave in the ruins of Komesu Castle, a heavy rain came. We couldn't cook rice because the water in the spring was too muddy. All we got was dry bread.

"I'll give this to my sisters' children and get potatoes from them," I thought. I visited the cave where my family was. My older sisters had one boy each. My oldest sister's boy was four. My next oldest sister's boy had just turned one. She was always carrying him on her back.

When I got there, I found several soldiers driving my family out of the cave. That was the cave my father dug for his family. It had taken him several days, and he left it for us when he was drafted into the Defense Corps.

I was surprised and said, "That's my family. Don't kick them out of our family cave." One of the soldiers shouted, "Why didn't you have them evacuated?"

My sisters' children were scared. They were almost crying because the soldiers were being so cruel. My mother and all my family members were forced out. Later I heard they headed for a natural cave on the beach saying, "If we're going to die anyway, let's go somewhere with clean air." A cave on the beach would be found easily by US ships. And in fact, my mother and all the others were killed there. That day was the last time I saw my family.

have them." He handed me thin leather woman's belt and a tin sewing box. The belt would later save my life. But a belt was new to me, so I fastened it over my *monpe* work pants.

The following night, his battalion left in the dark. I was happy, thinking I could go home. A soldier who had stayed behind said, "Don't leave the cave." They had left a "monitor" because they suspected we would leave the cave and ask the enemy for help.

Several days later Globe Brigade arrived.

We were ordered to stand in line in front of a warrant officer with a mustache. I gathered my courage and begged, "The battle is getting so intense. I would like to die with my parents. Please let us go home."

He looked fierce and shouted, "You worked for the Mountain Division but you don't want to work for us?!"

I learned later that they included us in their "army supplies," handing us over to the next unit regardless of our will.

This "Globe Brigade" included a few soldiers as young as 14 or 15 from the Homeland Protection Corps. Looking at their slender shoulders carrying ammunition boxes, I couldn't help feeling sorry for them. I was thinking, "Children like these are forced into the war?"

A few days after "Globe Brigade" came to Yamagusuku Village, the shelling became even more fierce. The brigade decided to abandon the cave in the village. We moved to a cave dug by the Warrior Division behind the ruins of Komesu Castle. That cave was strong and even had a tunnel.

Meanwhile, Shuri was captured by the US. Injured soldiers and refugees took shelter in our cave, turning it into a field hospital. They were carried in one after another. There were too many to accommodate, so quite a few lay down at the foot of the mountain.

We had no nurse and only one army surgeon. Surgery in the cave

Mountain Division. There, I found four of my friends (Kazu, Nobu, Shige and Fumi) already working for the division. We stayed in a cave during the day because of artillery from ships and bombing raids. We spent that time refining brown rice by pounding it with mortar and pestle. At night we went out to get water and pick vegetables.

We went to a spring about 300 meters from the cave to get water. My friends came, too, from other caves. I looked forward to seeing them, but we couldn't talk much. We couldn't even tell each other which units we were in. That was considered "espionage" and we would be scolded. We always had a soldier watching us to make sure we didn't talk too much.

Sometimes it was dangerous to work at night. An enemy plane would drop a flare. Then other flares would go up from the ground, and the area lit up like midday. A Grumman plane would then appear from somewhere and start straffing the area.

One night before we went to work, I was looking up at the sky from the entrance to the cave. A Japanese kamikaze plane appeared to the northeast. Then, suddenly, several enemy searchlights lit it up, and it was quickly shot down by antiaircraft guns.

After that, I saw no more kamikaze planes. Instead, I saw enemy Grumman fighters in huge formations filling the sky. When a pilot saw people moving down below, he would swoop down low and fire his machine gun. It was risking my life just to go to the latrine.

Looking out at the ocean, I saw US landing crafts near the island. Beyond them were battleships and aircraft carriers here and there. I heard the coast was full of enemy vessels not only at Komesu Beach where I was, but off the East and West coasts as well.

One evening a soldier was getting rid of his belongings. He called me and said, "My unit is leaving. I don't need these anymore, so you can to 30 Grumman bombers coming in from the ocean.

They dropped incendiary bombs one after another on the sugar-cane fields that spread fresh and green as far as I could see. Fire instantly spread all through the fields, causing tremendous crackling and popping. This was the first combat I saw.

Our legs were weak with fear, but we managed to get home. Other family members had already run to our air-raid shelter. My sister and I hurried to the shelter.

After noon the next day, the US started a full scale attack. We were unable to take a step out of the shelter because of fierce bombardment from the sea. The shells would hit with loud, terrifying booms.

At night it got quiet, so we went home to get some food. In our village no house was left standing. Some had burned. Others were rubble. We gave up on food and returned to the shelter. One evening a few days later, a deputy mayor visited our community and said, "US troops will be landing near the southern town of Yaese. Take refuge in Yanbaru forest (to the north)." We all raced to the north.

My family fled to Yonagusuku. It took several days to get there, and we failed to find a cave to hide in. We ended up hiding on the mountain during the day, waiting for nightfall. Then we went back to our cave in the village. Two old ladies with bad legs had been left behind in the village. They were extremely happy to see us come back. They must have felt completely helpless on their own.

One day, a few Japanese soldiers came to our cave and said, "How can we win the battle if young people like you stay home with your parents? Come help the army!" They took me away. Looking back now, that was the beginning of my great misfortune.

I was taken to Yamagusuku Village, the headquarters of the

working for an agricultural cooperative.

In 1944 the Warrior Division of the Kwantung Army (Japanese forces headquartered in Manchuria) entered Okinawa and started building fortifications and airfields. The men in the village were drafted for airfield construction and lived at the worksite.

Single women 25 or younger, like me, lived in airfield lodgings in Oroku and picked up rocks broken by dynamite, put them in bamboo colanders, and carried them on our heads. Students were mobilized, so nearly all villagers carried shovels and worked to build the airfield as quickly as possible.

Japan lost most of its aircraft carriers in the Battle of Midway in 1942 and was pressed by necessity to make Okinawa's southwest islands an air base. Plans called for airfields to be constructed at 15 locations.

Later, the Warrior Division was transferred to Taiwan and the Mountain Division came from Manchuria to replace them. The first major air raid on Okinawa took place on October 10, 1944. The town of Naha was burned to the ground. We had air raids frequently after that. We ran to air-raid shelters every time the siren sounded.

The shadow of war gradually grew darker and darker in Komesu, Itoman Village where I lived. School buildings became soldiers' barracks, and students were forced to study under trees.

Women took turns cooking for soldiers in the barracks. Since I was working for the agricultural cooperative, I was busy shipping vegetables to the army.

Early in the morning of March 23, 1945, on the way back from the well where I was getting water with my sister, we saw a formation of 20

Okinawa 1944-1945

I lost my left arm and my youth to a direct hit

Fumiko Tokumoto
Born August 1924. Worked for an agricultural cooperative at the time of the Battle of Okinawa. Father was drafted into the Defense Corps, so she lived with her mother and sisters in Itoman Village. She took refuge in a cave with her family but was taken to the headquarters of Mountain Division to work in the kitchen. The rest of her family was later driven from the cave by Japanese soldiers and killed, except her youngest sister. She and four friends resigned themselves to being killed and stayed in the headquarters cave. Her left arm was badly injured when a shell hit the cave. The arm was later amputated. Her friends were also injured and eventually died of those injuries. She reunited with her younger sister after the war. She kept telling herself, "My body is like this because of war," as she worked at a distribution center. Ninety-two years old, living in Itoman City.

Covered with blood, I escaped because my friend told me to

I have been asked many times, "Would you share your experience during the Battle of Okinawa?" But I have always declined. Every time I bring back those unwanted memories, my mind sinks into the pain, and I can't do anything for several days.

I lost my left arm in that battle, but I lost far more than that. Nothing is as foolish as war. And yet, wars continue. When I think about that reality, I feel unbearably powerless. Because of my desire to stop war, I started talking, little by little, about my war experience, mostly to junior high and high school students.

Itoman Village was a sugarcane area. Huge sugarcane farms were all around, and a sugar refinery was nearby. I was twenty years old,

March 24	US fleet opens artillery fire on Okinawa Island.
March 26	US troops land on Zamami and two neighboring islands. Residents on Geruma and Zamami islands commit mass suicide.
March 27	US troops land on three more islands, including Tokashiki.
March 28	Mass suicide on Tokashiki Island
End of March	Students in 21 Okinawa middle schools mobilized as "Iron Blood Student Corps for Emperor" and sent to front.
April 1	US troops land at Chatan and Yomitan villages on the west coast of Okinawa Island.
April 3	US army divides Okinawa Island; deploys troops north and south.
April 19	US troops break defensive line between Ginowan and Urasoe.
May 5	Japanese army fails all-out attack; defeat of Japanese army becomes certain.
May 22	Thirty-second Army Headquarters abandons Shuri and withdraws to south.
June 19	Thirty-second Army Commander Ushijima issues final order: "Fight bravely to the end and go to everlasting life for our cause." End of organized fighting
June 23	Commander Ushijima commits suicide.
June 25	Imperial Headquarters announces end of Okinawa Operation.
July 2	US Army declares end of Operation Iceberg.
August 15	Japan's unconditional surrender
September 7	US Army and Japanese Survival Unit sign instrument of surrender.

Chronology of the Battle of Okinawa

1944	
March 22	Japanese Imperial Headquarters establishes Thirty-second Army (Lieutenant General Masao Watanabe in command).
April 12	Thirty-second Army orders construction of an airfield on Ie Island in Okinawa.
July 7	Saipan falls.
August 10	Lt. General Mitsuru Ushijima replaces Watanabe as commander of Thirty-second Army.
August 22	Attacked by US submarine, student evacuation ship Tsushima-maru sinks near Akuseki Island; over 1480 killed, including about 780 students.
October 10	US task force conducts air raid on Nansei Islands; indiscriminate bombing of Naha burns 90 percent of city. (Note: Naha is the seat of the Okinawa Prefectural Government located in southwest corner of Okinawa Island)
December 9	Thirty-second Army starts building headquarters in cave under Shuri Castle. (Note: Shuri was capital of Ryukyu Kingdom (1429-1879))
December 14	Thirty-second Army forces Okinawa Prefectural Government to order all women and elderly residing in central or south Okinawa Island to evacuate north; all capable of fighting ordered to join battle under Nansei Islands Guard Guide line.
1945	
February 9	US Army launches Operation Iceberg.
February 10	Governor Akira Shimada directs 100,000 residents of central and south Okinawa Island to evacuate north.
March 23	US forces launch a full-scale attack on Okinawa Island.

CONTENTS

Preface 5

Chronology of the Battle of Okinawa 10

Fumiko Tokumoto 12

Nobu Tamashiro 22

Sumiko Tokuyama 28

Ume Oshiro 33

Mieko Izumikawa 38

Shizuko Maehara 50

Katsue Yonamine 57

Hiroko Kakazu 63

Reiko Kajiwara 69

Yoko Kamiyama 77

Hatsuko Arakawa 83

Mie Tanaka 95

Kikue Kaneshima 103

Hisako Yamagawa 111

In Closing 118

nature of authority."

We believe it important to keep in mind the inherent evil in militarist disrespect for civilians. When future generations look at the truth of the Battle of Okinawa, they will take great strides for peace and leave a better legacy for those to come. Our most cherished hope is that people around the world will read this book and let it guide them toward peace.

September 2016

Daigo Sunagawa
Chairman
Okinawa Youth Peace Committee

Yoshino Naka
Chairwoman
Okinawa Women's Peace and Culture Conference

were shocking, utterly inconceivable for young people with no war experience. In the course of their interviews, some told us they didn't want to relive these memories. We explained again the significance of this publication and persuaded them to continue. Other survivors were too old or infirm to share their experiences. Some even passed away before the scheduled interview.

On the other hand, several were in excellent health despite being over ninety years old. They shared their experiences effectively. In the process, we came to the painful realization that we have entered the final stage of the recording process. The opportunity to hear these war experiences directly from eyewitnesses will not be available much longer. We feel it is our duty or mission to pass on these experiences and the truth about the Battle of Okinawa.

In conclusion, we came to believe that the essence of the Battle of Okinawa was the uncontrollable evil of militarism. President Ikeda spoke to the First Okinawa Memorial General Assembly in the Okinawa Training Center in Onna Village on March 26, 1995, the fiftieth anniversary of the US landing in the Kerama Islands. He said:

"There is one point I want us to confirm together for the future. Nothing illustrates the fiendish nature of authority more than the Battle of Okinawa. Why did this battle take so many victims? Okinawa was made to suffer 'to defend the Japanese mainland. The strategy was to keep the US military bogged down in Okinawa as long as possible.' Okinawa was used as a shield, sacrificed for the sake of Japan's main islands …"

"The fiendish nature of authority is cruel. No one knows this as deeply in heart and soul as the people of Okinawa. That is why I began writing my novel *The Human Revolution* in this land, because Okinawa suffered most of all from the fiendish nature of authority. *The Human Revolution* depicts the struggles of ordinary people against the fiendish

We published five volumes of war testimony in the five years from June 1974 to June 1979. In 1981 we asked eyewitnesses to draw pictures of the Battle of Okinawa and collected about 700 works. We have held Battle of Okinawa picture exhibitions nationwide since 1985 to strengthen the spirit of peace. To extend this peace campaign into the future, seventy-one years after the end of the battle, on behalf of a new generation, we are publishing a new anti-war publication entitled *Okinawa 1944 - 1945 Thinking Peace for the Future—True Stories from 14 Survivors*.

Women and children always seem to suffer most in war. To highlight this phenomenon, we focused this time on women. Furthermore, most of the women we interviewed were children, younger than 20, when the Battle of Okinawa changed their lives forever.

We deliberately selected a wide variety of quite different experiences. Looking at the battle from many different angles is the best way to obtain a complete picture, and we believe this single book is remarkably comprehensive. One story involves running through a storm of artillery fire. Another survivor watched a Japanese soldier kill her brother. Others tell of the Himeyuri Student Corps, the mass suicides on Zamami and Geruma islands, a student evacuation ship sunk by a US submarine, and eyewitness testimony about conscripted Korean military laborers and comfort women.

Most people around the world know next to nothing about the Battle of Okinawa. But the world today is plagued by violent disputes and terrorist attacks. In this context, communicating the truth about the Battle of Okinawa takes on even greater importance. And to disseminate these testimonies beyond our borders, we present here a complete English translation.

The stories we heard from survivors of the Battle of Okinawa

Preface

The Soka Gakkai Student Division held a meeting at Okinawa Headquarters in Naha on December 2, 1964. SGI (Soka Gakkai International) President Daisaku Ikeda happened to be in Okinawa and attended that meeting. This unscheduled appearance was the first time the students had met the President.

President Ikeda spoke earnestly about Okinawa's peace-building mission: "Okinawa has had a tragic past. Its history has been like a tempest of negative karma. For that reason, it is from here that waves of peace and a breeze of happiness must emanate.

I hope that from among your ranks will emerge people of great capability who, proud of their Okinawa heritage, will lead Japan and the world."

Nine years later, we learned that President Ikeda started writing *The Human Revolution* that day in Okinawa. "Nothing is more barbarous than war.Nothing is more cruel...."

When members of the Soka Gakkai Okinawa Youth Division learned that President Ikeda started writing *The Human Revolution* on December 2, they became even more determined to publish their first volume of war testimony *The Shattered Uruma Island*.

The thesis of *The Human Revolution* is that "A great human revolution in just a single individual will help achieve a change in the destiny of a nation and further,will enable a change in the destiny of all humankind." The Soka Gakkai Okinawa Youth Division has long campaigned to convey memories of the Battle of Okinawa. The goal of this activity is to create ripples of peace and promote the "human revolution" throughout Japan and around the world.

Okinawa 1944-1945

**Thinking Peace for the Future
True Stories from 14 Survivors**

DAISANBUNMEI-SHA
TOKYO

Copyright © Soka Gakkai 2016

Published in Japan in 2016
by Daisanbunmei-sha,Inc.
1-23-5 Shinjuku Shinjuku-ku,Tokyo Japan
http://www.daisanbunmei.co.jp

未来へつなぐ平和のウムイ
──沖縄戦を生き抜いた14人の真実

2016年10月2日　初版第1刷発行

編　者	創価学会沖縄青年部
発行者	大島光明
発行所	株式会社　第三文明社 東京都新宿区新宿1-23-5 郵便番号：160-0022 電話番号：03（5269）7144（営業代表） 　　　　　03（5269）7145（注文専用） 　　　　　03（5269）7154（編集代表） 振替口座　00150-3-117823 URL http://www.daisanbunmei.co.jp
英語翻訳	澤田美和子
装幀・本文DTP	木村祐一（株式会社ゼロメガ）
印刷・製本	藤原印刷株式会社

©Soka Gakkai 2016　　　　　　　　　　Printed in Japan
ISBN978-4-476-06230-4

乱丁・落丁本はお取り換えいたします。ご面倒ですが、小社営業部宛お送りください。
送料は当方で負担いたします。
法律で認められた場合を除き、本書の無断複写・複製・転載を禁じます。